D0866820

BLAIKIE'S GUIDE TO MODERN MANNERS

Also by Thomas Blaikie

You Look Awfully Like the Queen:
Wit and Wisdom from the House of Windsor

BLAIKIE'S GUIDE
TO
MODERN MANNERS

Thomas Blaikie

FOURTH ESTATE • *London*

First published in Great Britain in 2005 by
Fourth Estate
An imprint of HarperCollins*Publishers*
77–85 Fulham Palace Road
London W6 8JB
www.4thestate.co.uk

1

A catalogue record for this book is
available from the British Library

ISBN 0–00–720301–2

Typeset in Minion by
Rowland Phototypesetting Ltd, Bury St Edmunds, Suffolk

Printed in Great Britain by Clays Ltd, St Ives plc

To my mother,
whose manners are a miracle

Acknowledgements

I was very lucky to have *two* editors for this book; first of all the brilliant and remarkable publisher, Christopher Potter, and then Silvia Crompton, who has made wonderful suggestions and been extraordinarily patient and efficient. It is unusual to be able to thank the publicity department at this stage, but Jessica Axe has made astonishing advances in promoting this book well before publication. Others who have confided their manners anxieties to me and been hugely helpful in all kinds of other ways are: Peter Parker, Adam Bager, Carol Clark, Kit Reading, Michael Knowles, David Newell, Rory Smith, Anthony Wilson, Nigel Spalding, Philip Hensher, Derek Granger, Elizabeth Burke, Bill Hamilton, Kate Parkin, Sarah Long, Joe Hunter, Alan Hollinghurst, Tom Adès, Julian Humphries, Ian Hay, Tim Hely Hutchinson, Sean Swallow, Martin Neild, Tessa Neild, Patrick O'Connor, Patric Dickinson, Tash Aw, Miles Barber, John Clinch, Alastair Hendy, Jane Seery, Ivan Seery, Mark Wilkinson, Annette Fynes-Clinton and Richard Walker.

Contents

Communications Manners

Let's Get Together: Inviting and Accepting Manners

Introduction

This is a guide to *modern* manners. You're bound to be wondering what's so modern about them and how they're different from old manners, which, if you're over forty-five, you'll remember. Old manners were not always very well mannered and had it in for certain defenceless groups. Children were not favoured, especially if sitting down. It was, 'Get up, a lady's come into the room,' 'Get up for your uncle/aunt/granny' or any senior person for that matter. In fact, children were lucky to get a seat at all and risked having it commandeered for no good reason by any nearby adult. Mealtimes weren't much fun for anybody because of *table manners*. Eaters had always to be in a state of sentry-like alertness in case somebody wanted the salt/pepper/water/ butter. It was a terrible mark of failure if they had to ask. To top it all, so worrying and complex were manners, they were just about the only topic of conversation. In the 1960s, the matron at a friend of mine's boarding school, eating as by custom with her eight-year-old charges, conducted a lively mealtime debate on a particularly awkward point: in what position on the plate should you leave your knife and fork when you had finished eating? Should it be six o'clock, four o'clock or nine o'clock? Should the prongs of the fork be turned up or down? This same matron decreed that nobody was to put their elbows on the table unless they were an uncle or over twenty-one. But obviously it was a different story entirely when a boy, claiming quite truthfully that he *was* an uncle, actually put his elbows on the table.

Scarcely a trace remains now of this bizarre labyrinthine world of 'manners'. 'Come as you are,' we say, 'be yourself.' The tables have turned so completely that it is now a fault, if not an affliction, to be too polite, too 'well-mannered'. Such people are dysfunctional, in need of therapy of some kind. 'If only they could relax,' we say, 'be more casual, less stuffy. Such a shame!'

We've got rid of all the crazy old rules, we can do what we like, wear what we like, turn up when we like and everything's completely and utterly wonderful, isn't it? We can do without manners.

Well, maybe not. Look at the way Tracey Emin, of all people, complained about nasty people who sniggered when some of her artworks were incinerated in the Momart fire: 'It is just not fair and it's not funny and it's not polite and *it's bad manners.*' (This the worst thing, coming climactically at the end.) And why, in the course of my research, did I find so much anxiety and guilt? At the merest mention of my subject people would invariably look at the ground. One woman, in her early twenties, even said, 'Are you looking at me to see what my manners are like?' This kind of thing was often a prelude to a torrent of enquiries: is it OK to thank by e-mail? Should I bring a bottle? What do I do about inviting estranged couples? What's a nice way to end a text-message conversation that's been going on just a bit too long?

This uncertainty turned out to have deeper implications. Far from seeing manners as superficial, a formality and a restraint on individuality and self-expression, a lot of people said that they would feel more themselves if they were more sure of their manners. As one woman put it, 'I hate it if I think I've done something ungenerous or gauche. I know it's just not me. I'm not a selfish or inconsiderate person.'

Our free-and-easy ways have left us in a vacuum of uncertainty and embarrassment. And this only gets worse because we are reluctant to give each other any guidance. If someone is late or doesn't reply to the invitation, we say it doesn't matter; if a friend won't stop talking on their mobile phone while we're out with them we make excuses, we say they probably don't realise what they're doing, they don't mean any harm. We'll just have to go on seething inside. We don't think it's our place to judge or tell other people what to do, but who knows? Maybe those other people are as worried about their manners as we are about ours? Maybe they have a nasty uneasy feeling of *having got away with it.* Nothing more than that.

Many people take damaging avoiding action rather than confront the problem. Let's *not* have a party. It's too humiliating when half the intended guests don't answer the invitation and the other half say they'll come but either don't show up at all or arrive at least two hours after the whole miserable occasion is supposed to have started. Let's *not* invite people round mid-week. They'll all come at least an hour late and then never leave. We'll have to crawl through the rest of the week on our hands and knees with exhaustion.

It's time to act before we descend into anarchy and inner paralysis, and social life dwindles to nothing. What we need are modern manners. You can have modern manners without turning into Colonel Blimp strutting up and down and finding fault. Modern manners aren't old manners. Modern manners are rational and liberating. They say, 'Do what makes sense,' and forget the rest. Don't worry about things that don't matter very much. It's extraordinary how many people are *still* anxious about which cutlery to use (according to Cecil Beaton even the Queen Mother glanced anxiously to see what others were doing), how to pronounce certain words, what to wear. The British, especially, live in unnecessary dread of giving offence and not being good enough. If I take a bottle, will the hosts be offended? We couldn't possibly ask them back, they're such marvellous cooks and we can only manage M & S. And then there's guilt – I'd better drag on and on with this phone call because I don't quite like to say I've got something else I need to do urgently.

Let's be free of all this. It's so much easier to 'move on' at a party, or to end one of those exchanges of text messages that could go on for ever, if you can get rid of the guilt.

Why feel guilty? It's quite natural to want to talk some of the *other* people at the party, and conversations have got to come to an end at some point.

And while we're about it, there's another prison we could break out of. Why not say, 'Actually, it's not absolutely perfect and ideal and wonderful that you're an hour late/never replied to the invitation/said you'd come but didn't.' Modern manners mean you can find nice cheerful ways of casting off the shallow mask of manner. Say what you really think. Be bold. And when your friends all turn up on time for your party because you've rather suggested that they might and the whole thing gets going with a swing and everybody's happy, they'll thank you for it.

Manners in Public

Where to begin? 'Good morning,' 'Thank you,' pushing and shoving – among other things

Dreadful, dreadful – let's rave on like Colonel Blimp, such fun! It's frightful out on the streets. Surely a new Ice Age of bad manners is nigh? There are the litter bugs, the pushers and shovers, the bellowers, the swearers – and that's just a start.

What about this dreadful episode? The other day Matt Lawson, forty-three, assistant financial director of a company that publishes trade magazines (*Dumper Truck Today* is a big seller) held the door open for a nice, middle-aged, vaguely spinsterish woman as she was coming out of a department store in Peterborough and, would you believe it, she stalked straight through the door as if there was nobody there?

Matt says this happens all the time, not just in Peterborough but also in London where he works. 'It would be nice if they said thank you,' he says, 'but what can you do? That's how people are.'

In the genteel cathedral city of Worcester a similar thing happened. Some ladies failed to thank someone who had waited for them to come up a narrow stairs. In Manchester and London, queuing for the bus has been abandoned in favour of a dog-eat-dog approach.

Mrs Gibbs, eighty-five, lives in Winchester, her husband, a solicitor, long dead. 'I don't want to seem old-fashioned,' she begins. 'But I'm sorry to say, people are in such a hurry. All these mothers with one child in a pushchair, several more rampaging about. They've got no time to take any notice of anybody. People hold doors open for me, that kind of thing. They can see I'm an old woman. But the other day I thanked someone and he grunted in this peculiar way as if to say, "That's enough of that. I've done you a favour, now clear off!" Not terribly charming.'

And what about this? One of those van-type vehicles in which celebrities are conveyed was once seen parked outside a tailor's in Spitalfields. A rumour, unconfirmed to this day, went round that David Beckham was being fitted for a suit. The van was assumed to be unoccupied except by the driver but imagine the excitement when the back door slid open and a jewelled hand, clutching a coke can and associated sandwich wrappings, emerged into view, sank graciously towards the gutter and there deposited the can. Could this have been the hand of Posh, glamorously littering the streets?

What shall we do with them? Horsewhipping? Boot camp? National Service?

Well, it may not be the end of the world, but, let's admit

it, we've all got something, some discourtesy that occurs in public, which we find *absolutely infuriating.*

It's no good resigning yourself, like Matt, or apologising, like Mrs Gibbs. You've got to do something, especially if you're one of the millions who complain about antisocial behaviour (now an *election* issue, as we have seen). You can't expect the police to attend every time someone drops some litter or raises their voice.

The good old British 'keep your head down and don't make a fuss' approach has had its day. Not that it ever really was that. Nothing may have been said, but the accompanying *withering looks* were full strength and top-notch in quality. Actors would have given anything to achieve such silent power. But nobody today is going to take any notice of a look, however withering.

· If you hold a door open for someone or wait to let them pass and they don't thank you, say loudly, 'Thank you so much.' In exteme cases you can pursue them and say, 'I'm so sorry. Did you forget to thank?' Don't be put off by an abusive response. If enough people start doing this, the message will get through.

- If you're the person not thanking, you probably don't mean any harm. You're just not awake.

- Always say, 'Good morning,' 'Hello,' or 'Hi,' to shop assistants, receptionists etc. The French do this without thinking about it. In some places, you'll be met with astonishment or bewilderment. Don't be discouraged. It's the right thing to do.

- If there's no queue for the bus, just a scrum, it would be nice to think that enough people would band together to do something about it. But they probably won't. Nevertheless there are other ways of making a fuss. Write to the local paper, complain to the council, your MP, the bus company. Don't listen to people who sneer at the

British and their eternal queues. Queues are fair and just. They're worth fighting for.

- In a crowd, few follow the example of the late Bubbles Rothermere who would beat the back of anyone in the way with her tiny fists. But many have a policy of massively increasing speed and biffing everybody else out of the way. This isn't very nice but is less easy to resist. They've usually disappeared by the time you realise what has happened. Protest charmingly – 'I'm so sorry. I didn't realise I was in the way' – if you get the chance. Or just don't get out of the way. Stand your ground and see what happens.

- If you see someone dropping litter, pick it up and hand it back to them. 'I think you dropped this.' It sometimes works. If they turn nasty, say, 'It's quite all right. I'll throw it away for you.' Then make a run for it.

Children

In public places there are two sorts: ones who are unaccompanied, ones who aren't. Neither are quite as they should be. 'I was in the newsagents only last week,' says Mrs Gibbs. 'Two little boys, both under ten, rushed in making an awful noise, barged in front of me and shouted at the shopkeeper, "Give us some chewing gum." I wasn't going to stand there doing nothing, I can tell you. I said, "Stop that racket, wait in the queue, if you wouldn't mind, and when it's your turn you might try 'Please' and 'Thank you'." The shopkeeper and the one other customer in the shop were horrified. "You ought to watch out," they said, "they might have had a gun." I couldn't believe it. What nonsense! Three adults in the shop and two little boys and the only person who wasn't afraid of them an old woman of eighty-five!'

At the airport, setting out with a party of ten for a villa holiday in Majorca, Zoe Miller, 25, just starting out in PR and a graduate of the University of Kent (one of those subjects that are hard to explain), was fed up with 'all these parents who seemed to think the departure lounge was just a big play-pen for their children. One of the fathers was making the most noise, pretending to be a roller-coaster or something.' Zoe is rather against children in general, which Mrs Gibbs isn't. But perhaps Zoe has a point. It probably wasn't just thoughtlessness either. Many parents now like to make a conspicuous parade of their parenting and what better opportunity than the departure lounge?

Did she do anything about it? She is shocked. 'Oh, no. That wouldn't be right, would it? I'm not a busybody. It's just my personal opinion that they're annoying.'

Zoe's not thinking straight. She's being too nice. It isn't 'just my personal opinion'. She's got a fair point. A public space is a public space. It isn't for one special interest group to take over.

- If unaccompanied children are behaving inconsiderately in public – making a lot of noise, dropping litter, barging queues – intervene if it is safe to do so and you are likely to get somewhere, in other words if there is a majority of adults present.

- Speak firmly but politely.
- Most children, even 'well-brought-up' ones, will take advantage if they sense that adults are afraid of them.
- Most 'antisocial behaviour' is perpetrated by children and teenagers. If adults won't step in to put a stop to minor outbreaks it isn't very surprising that some young people will graduate to more advanced forms.
- Parents of small children: it may be difficult to keep your offspring amused, especially if waiting in a public place, but try to show consideration for others. Once, at a rather serious concert, I sat in front of a child who had been supplied with a rattly teddy to keep her occupied for the duration.

- You're more likely to get people's backs up if your underlying attitude seems to be that your child has a *right* to rampage about. If you are apologetic and make some attempt to restrain, you will get a more indulgent response.

- If you are exasperated by unfettered children (e.g. strange child actually crawling over you in a café; mother looking on waiting for you to coo admiration) *you're going to have to say something.* Don't be relativist; don't think, 'Who am I to tell others what to do?' Stand up for what you believe in!

Get a move on: cashpoints and checkouts

'Why don't people know how to use a cashpoint machine?' Zoe asks. In the queue she becomes impatient. But she is not quite herself near a cash dispenser anyway – so many anxieties about lack of funds. She'd rather snatch the smallest sum she thinks she can get away with and run. Which is why, in the supermarket, she is often holding up the queue paying £6.78 on her debit card and annoying people like Matt, always in a hurry because of family commitments. If you probe deeper into Matt's soul, you'll find that he does sometimes wonder why so many people stand for twenty minutes in a queue at the checkout and *still haven't got their money ready.*

- Try to achieve technical mastery of the cashpoint machine. If there is a queue, don't go on and on trying to make it give you money when you know quite well your account is empty. If you have a complicated transaction, apologise to anybody you are keeping waiting.
- Perhaps one day, in supermarkets, there will be a queue for people who have got their money or their cards ready.

- To speed things up, hand over your card as soon as all your goods have been scanned. Don't wait until you have finished packing them.
- Don't keep everybody waiting while you spend hours devising some gargantuan Dewey decimal system for packing your purchases.

Munch as you go and What's that smell?

'Don't get me wrong,' says Mrs Gibbs. 'I wouldn't want to go back to the old days, when you got a withering look for sucking on a throat lozenge in Woolworth's. But this eating on the street does seem to have got out of hand. People are working their way through whole hot dinners.'

Perhaps she exaggerates just a little. But Zoe, young and carefree, is frequently to be seen in her lunch hour waving a plastic fork in one hand and holding a tinfoil tray full of carrot salad in the other – with not a few bits of carrot trailing on the pavement behind her. Others wield enormous door-step sandwiches and rolls whose contents are a challenge to control.

Then on the trains and buses you see people tucking in to fish-and-chip dinners, curry suppers, sweet-and-sour pork, spare ribs. London Transport thought there was enough of a problem in 2004 to launch an anti-smelly-food poster campaign featuring an Italian-looking man hung about with salamis and bits of Parma ham. This caused grave offence. The Italian ambassador was obliged to point out that these foods are not smelly.

Be that as it may, eating on the hoof isn't very good for you and shows the minimum of respect for food. But that's not the point. The old-fashioned idea that it just wasn't dainty to eat in public might have been absurd but:

- The sight of people gnawing on huge filled rolls or trying awkwardly to eat chop suey from a tinfoil tray while walking along is rarely attractive.
- If you are struggling to eat this kind of food on the street, you are very likely to be in the way.
- In enclosed spaces, some people will think that what you're eating smells horrible.
- Good walking food can be chocolate, ice cream, lollies, modestly filled sandwiches.
- If you want a picnic, why not find somewhere to sit down and have it properly?

May I have your seat?

Some years ago, as an experiment for a TV programme, researchers trawled a railway carriage asking if they could have people's seats. In the majority of cases the answer was yes, sometimes even though there were empty seats all around. This was supposed to prove the innate tendency of human beings to obey orders. 'I wish I'd known when I was younger,' says Mrs Gibbs. 'It's all right now that I'm unmistakably ancient, but when I was in my late sixties and we lived in London, I'd be desperate for a seat sometimes, struggling back from John Lewis with ten new pillows.' But she didn't like to ask – in fact, she wanted to be offered – and so she didn't get one. The same thing happens to others, most notably pregnant women. In this case would-be givers-up of seats dread making a mistake – offering a seat to someone who's just a bit stout. Transport for London have identified this as a serious problem and plan to issue pregnant women with badges saying 'Baby on Board' – but not everybody is so keen on this idea. On the TV news they tried out the badges and found they worked a treat.

By and large people who might give up their seats seem to be paralysed with embarrassment.

There is also the vexed question of seated children. The thinking today is that they are to remain enthroned at all costs. Is this right? 'It's annoying when some little tot's got a seat and I have to stand,' says Zoe. But can she be relied on, being generally anti-child?

- Some older people may not look it but they may still need your seat (if carrying a lot of shopping, generally appearing at the end of their tether etc.). Give it to them.
- Don't let anxiety that they will feel insulted ('Do I look that old?') hold you back.
- If you think a woman might be pregnant, give her your seat. If you've made a mistake, it won't matter. After all, she'll never know *why* you gave up your seat, and if she's got any sense she'll be glad to get one even if slightly insulted.
- If you badly need a seat and nobody is offering, ask. Of course it would be nicer to be offered, but at least, if the

results of that experiment are anything to go by, you're quite certain of success.

· On the whole we should give up our seats more often.

Are children never to give up their seats on public transport? They should not be pitched out, old-style, just because they are children. But if an entire family is seated and an elderly person is standing, does it not make sense for one of the children to relinquish its seat? Being smaller and younger, are they not better suited to standing? Can't very small children share? Isn't this often what they are doing anyway? Or running around not even occupying 'their' seats?

Not satisfied

Mrs Gibbs went once with her nephew to Sorrento. 'I couldn't believe it. He didn't like his room in the hotel so he asked for another. I'd never have dared.' This is the traditional British 'don't make a fuss' approach taken to extremes. But Matt, almost half Mrs Gibbs's age, isn't much better. 'I don't like complaining,' he says. He tells a story of getting one of those bargain first class deals on Eurostar and a 'ludicrous woman' who made a terrible fuss because the attendant allowed someone to sit in her seat while she was in the bar. 'She was away for hours and everyone thought she'd got off. When she came back the person gave her her seat back immediately but still she had to complain. She kept on saying over and over again, "It's not what you expect *in first class*." The whole point was to tell everyone that she was in first class but we all knew that because we were there too. My wife Lucy thought it was very funny but I wished the woman would belt up.'

Zoe, on the other hand, is an unhesitant complainer and really rather good at it.

- If you have reason to be dissatisfied, you should complain. You are paying after all.
- If you complain in a public place, such as a hotel lobby, a railway carriage or a restaurant, you will almost certainly have an audience although you might not know it. People nearby will be listening in.
- For this reason a lot of people take a huge amount of trouble – staging their complaints as if they were giving a presentation at work or reprimanding an employee in the modern manner, i.e. constructively, with huge emphasis on the positive, suggestions for the future etc. On the whole this is a good thing, but be careful you're not making a mountain out of a molehill. There's no need to spend ten elaborate minutes going through all the strong points of your hotel room as a prelude to asking if the bedside lamp could be fixed.

Tipping

'Why do we have to have tipping?' says Zoe, for whom the occasional taxi is quite expensive enough. She's right, of course. It's patronising and drives everyone into a frenzy of indignation and anxiety – who to tip? How much? Why?

In theory, a tip is given for personal services beyond the call of duty. It is supposed to be freely given. In practice, punters compensate for meagre salaries and if they don't they're punished in ways too terrifying to think about.

Tipping gives unfair advantages. Very rich people ensure good service by wisely distributing £50 notes *on arrival* in hotels and restaurants.

There is no rationale to tipping. You wouldn't think of tipping the person at Tesco's who helps you find the frozen peas.

The whole thing stinks. In Iceland tipping is outlawed.

But we are lumbered with it.

- Black-cab drivers in London are tipped 10 per cent – a practice which should have been discontinued long ago. They earn good money. They don't need a tip.
- The custom of tipping has never taken root in the minicab world. You agree a price at the start of the journey and that's it. Don't for goodness' sake start tipping minicab drivers.
- Restaurants usually add a 12.5 per cent service charge. This isn't a tip but an extra charge although you can withhold it. Only do this if you are absolutely sure the poor service was the waiter's fault. Most people feel sorry for waiters since they are poorly paid.
- If you pay the service charge it is not necessary to leave any further tip.
- Some people tip hairdressers. This is absurd. Nowadays hairdressers are glamorous professionals. You wouldn't

tip your child's teacher or your lawyer, so why tip the hairdresser?

- Porters in hotels have to be tipped for carrying your suitcases to your room – annoying when you have just arrived and only have a 100-euro note. The usual tip is a couple of pounds or euros.

- If someone has provided really exceptional service over a long period (a waiter, hotel staff, a coach driver or builder perhaps), it would be far more personal and less patronising to give them a present. At one time 'grateful patients' used to give their doctors expensive presents. Lawyers too would often get cases of wine or cigars. But now everybody hates doctors and lawyers. If you were *really* grateful, you could lavish something choice upon them (see – **Presents: It's the thought that counts**, page 222).

At the leisure centre or gym

Mrs Gibbs gave up the public swimming pool in her mid-seventies because she was afraid of being mown down in the water. Matt and Zoe are both dilatory attenders at gyms. Matt only goes when he has to stay down in London for the evening for some reason; otherwise he is rushing back to his wife and children in Peterborough. Besides, he complains that his gym is full of 'rather aggressive types'. We know what he means: usually men, scowling, banging away at the machines, breathing in and out in a noisy and conspicuously efficient way, allowing others to have a go with bad grace. Some of them never put the free weights back in the right place and, sweating being a proud feature, leave horrible sweat patches all over the machines. At Zoe's council-run gym, women-only evenings have been introduced to counteract this problem. Not that this entirely suits her, since she sees the gym as a good opportunity to meet men and indeed has come across a number of boyfriends in this way.

- Gyms and swimming pools are social places; many of them are indeed clubs.
- If your idea is to be 'totally focused' on your own fitness programme and to resent any 'distractions', perhaps you should take up some solitary form of exercise such as round-the-world yachting.
- It is not unreasonable to assume that members of the same gym will smile at each other and exchange the odd friendly word.
- Allow others to use a machine while you rest between sets – this is called 'working in'.
- Don't 'reserve' a machine by putting a towel on the seat before wandering off for a prolonged chat with someone on the other side of the room.
- Put equipment back in the right place and wipe down machines after you've used them.
- A great deal of 'picking up' and 'chatting up' goes on in gyms (as it does in libraries). Disapproving of this is priggish and pointless – what else would anyone expect when a lot of youngish people with few clothes on are working up a sweat together?

- If you have to turn somebody down, try to nice about it (see **Chatting up, dating, turning down**, page 186).
- A gym is one of the few places where straight men may gaze at themselves in the mirror without risk of being mistaken for gay – not that gay men would ever waste time in that way, of course.

Drunkenness

We hear a lot about binge drinking and most of it is true. Pleasant cathedral cities, such as St Albans and Winchester, turn into hellholes on Friday and Saturday nights. Even Mrs Gibbs, eighty-five, is fully clued up. 'I have a friend who lives next to a camping barn in Devon. Once it was occupied by some lawyers – all men – who were so drunk they threw all the furniture and things like the microwave into the river. Another time it was some young people who'd just finished their A levels. They ended up on the roof hurling abuse.'

There is much debate about whether all this isn't just traditional British behaviour and nothing to make a fuss about. Traditional or not, it isn't very nice. In its present form, drunkenness seems to be no respecter of class. Matt complains that his train home to Peterborough is frequently stopped for drunks to be expelled: 'You see some City type in a suit out of his mind on the platform.' Aggression and violence also are new features. The pre-war days of Bertie Wooster and Gussie Finknottle getting rather squiffy and stealing policemen's helmets have gone for good. Even Zoe, many of whose friends are up for the Friday-night blow-out, has noticed it. 'Last New Year's Eve I had to walk home most of the way to Balham from the West End. The only people I saw were blind drunk. Every single one of them was either weeping hysterically, shouting really aggressively at the bouncers outside a pub or club, or they were couples having horrible rows.'

Or the severely inebriated person ends up alone – like Euan Blair, lying abandoned by his mates in the gutter. But encountering the Prime Minister across the table in the police station later is not usually part of the experience.

· For the sake of others, don't get blind drunk.

Mobile phones in public places

Mrs Gibbs, travelling on a train (first class at a knock-down pensioner rate), complained of a young man 'bellowing into a phone for nearly an hour, trying to book a hotel room in Finland'.

On buses, on trains, in shops, everywhere, mobile phones are a nuisance, aren't they? It isn't just the ring tones – *why are all of them silly?* – it's the sword clash of different conversations conducted at full volume: while one person is blaring away about last night's sex, another is having a huge set-to with their insurance company about a minor car accident, and a third is nit-picking their way through the discounts on offer from Thomas Cook – 'If we go out on the third and return on the fourteenth . . . but how about going out on the fifth and coming back on the twelfth?' etc.

The solution is easy – so why has no one thought of it?

- YOU DON'T NEED TO SHOUT. When phones were first invented people thought they had to shout into them, since the people they were talking to were far away. But, after almost 130 years, we ought to know better.
- As for nightmare ring tones, whatever happened to 'vibrating alert'? No phone needs to ring in a public place. So why do they? It's this frenzied anxiety, again, isn't it? My wife might be calling to announce that she's planning a quiche for supper or it might be one of the children demanding to know why there are no more Skittles. IT CAN WAIT.
- It really is impolite to be on the phone while paying for things in shops. Calm down. One thing at a time. Make your call quietly in a corner, then pay. Don't be in such a hurry. If the phone rings *while* you are paying, ignore it. You are dealing with the person on the till. That comes first.
- Witnesses to the above should apologise loudly to the shop worker on the rude person's behalf.
- Mobile mobile phone users (as it were) are always in the way. Walking along the pavement, getting off a train and so on, they don't know where they are or what they're doing. These people should be tucked away behind pillars, seated in designated seating areas; they should be OUT OF THE WAY. Why aren't they?

Chance encounters

An innocent walk down the street can turn into a nightmare
when somebody you're sure you've never seen before claims
to know you. This happens frequently to Matt. At one time
he was frightened to go out of his office at lunch-time. Or
you might vaguely recognise the person trying to speak to
you, but that's about it.

- If you have no recollection whatsoever of the person,
  you're going to have to grin and bear it. All being well,
  the stranger before you will have given you a handle,
  however fragile – the names of your mutual acquaintances, perhaps – to cling on to.
- Don't say, 'I'm afraid I can't remember your name.' People
  don't like being forgotten. It is a kindness to conceal your
  ignorance – even where it is obvious, with nothing being
  said, that the other person *knows* that you haven't the
  first idea who they are. As Quentin Crisp put it, 'Most
  people would rather be treated courteously than be told
  the truth.'
- If you are the forgotten one, don't say, 'You don't remember me, do you?' because however you say it it will sound
  like a criticism.
- Being embarrassed about being embarrassed is imprison-
  ing. Liberate yourself with low expectations. Reconcile
  yourself to awkwardness from the start to the finish of
  these chance encounters.
- There ought to be some ungainly banter. 'Hi, how are

you?' isn't enough. Revel in the ghastliness. Expect nothing more than clichés and discomfort. Alternatives might well be condemned as 'slick' and 'artificial', anyway. Don't forget that there's always the chance of something better . . . romance, perhaps.

- It is perfectly all right for one of you to take the initiative in saying goodbye, but a tendency is creeping in for this to be done in a practised and 'professional' manner – more a matter of tone than what is said. It is best if you can remain as bumbling and ill at ease as possible. Ideally, there should be several attempts to part, with conversation spluttering to life again in between.

Neighbours

Have the soap operas, particularly the one of this section's name, put people off being neighbourly? If you start speaking to the neighbours you will certainly end up sleeping with most of them and marrying quite a few. Rumours about your sexuality will start flying around and you'll have to do some more sleeping around to prove the contrary. Roughly every four years you will be the victim of a con man. In the years when you are not a victim of a con man one of the following will be bound to happen: you will be wrongly accused of either murder or major fraud, never both; your house will burn down; you will trip over a paving stone and successfully sue the council; you will disappear overseas, never to be heard of again.

It's neighbourly where Matt lives, in a nice new-build in

Peterborough. At Christmas time, they're in and out of each other's houses, having drinks; the mothers share the school run and there's a summer party. But elsewhere it's a different story. 'Some years ago, I was struggling to get a bag of manure in and a neighbour rushed out of his house to help me,' says Mrs Gibbs, who lives in one of a row of Victorian cottages in Winchester. 'But whenever I've seen that man subsequently – not a flicker. I seem to have become invisible.'

People are peculiar. There have been other cases of neighbours steadfastly refusing to pop next door for a cup of tea or even a meal, possibly because their own house is a tip and they dread having to ask back. In other cases, hospitality is accepted but never returned. Some people avoid their neighbours on principle, dreading being stuck with them if they so much as exchange a word.

Zoe's street in Balham is not very neighbourly but this may be to do with her habit of putting the rubbish out on the wrong day. There's also the matter of her noisy parties . . .

- 'Love thy neighbour as thyself' – neighbourliness is more than good manners, it is a virtue, a mark of goodness.
- It doesn't matter if your neighbours are dull or even a nuisance – they are your neighbours. You have something in common.
- Don't shun your neighbours out of mean-spiritedness – jealousy over their decor, dread of having to ask back, fear of being lumbered. This is nonsense.
- If you accept hospitality from your neighbours, which

you should, don't forget to ask them back (see **Do we dare to ask them back?**, page 132).

- Ignoring your neighbours or, even worse, ignoring them *after* you have spoken once or twice, is unkind and hostile. They will assume that they have given offence or that you look down on them in some way. They will be hurt.
- Noise is a serious business. Loud music, banging doors, shouting etc. can cause real distress. There is the thing itself but also the feeling of being trampled all over, not shown any consideration, as well as the anxiety over whether it's ever going to stop.
- Respond readily to any requests to make less noise.
- If you are planning a party with music, check with neighbours well in advance ('We hope you won't mind' etc.) and give them accurate information about how long you are proposing to play music for. Invite them to the party.

The laying of flowers

Many shrines are seen by the wayside now. People lay flowers at the scenes of fatal accidents. Elsewhere, tributes are left in spots special in some way to a departed loved one or at the scenes of murders. Mrs Gibbs is suspicious. 'My friend lives at a beauty spot in Devon. People leave flowers but they never come and clear them away when they're over, and often they leave the plastic wrapping on. I'm also rather against the whole thing, I'm sorry to say. It's not terribly encouraging, at my age, having all these reminders of death all over the place. And some of these roadside shrines – they go on and on, don't they?'

- If you are laying flowers in a public place, remove the plastic wrapping. Return to take away the dead flowers.
- Permanent shrines are hard on the living, especially if beside roads or near houses. After six months they should be removed. Thereafter, they can be resurrected on the anniversary of the death that occurred there, provided that the flowers are removed when dead.

Work Manners

What are work manners?

A lot of people loathe automatic answering services ('Please choose from the following eighteen options') or shops where the assistants are more interested in choosing the next CD track than serving the customers. But what might look like bad manners is really bad business. There was an absurd clothes shop in London called Voyage that, rudely, wouldn't let just anyone in. You had to be invited. Quite rightly, it went out of business.

Equally, good manners at work can be skin deep – adopted, often after going on a course of some kind, simply for personal advancement. Why has so-and-so suddenly started offering to help the boss's PA with the flowers for the foyer? Or taken to making a sympathy call every time the MD is ill?

Here we look at manners that have nothing to with success or failure at work. These manners, when adopted, just make the workplace a better place to be.

Greetings

In ordinary life, deliberately ignoring someone you know, 'blanking' them, is a devastating act of full-scale hostility. But at work, so some people think, it's a feather in your cap. 'Look at me,' they seem to say as they stump by, busy, busy, without a glimmer of recognition, 'I'm so useful and important I've not got a moment to spare.' This is what it's like at Matt's office – grim. People have got their heads down, they're far too busy wondering how many column inches to devote to innovations in gear-box design on dumper trucks. They couldn't possibly say hello. Zoe does at least say hi to the people of her own age in her PR agency, but strangely has no greeting for her managing director when she goes into her office to tell her how well she's getting on with some new press contact.

- Nothing is more dismal than a workplace where people don't greet each other.
- Greet people *the first time you see them that day* (however late it is) and *before* you launch into whatever business you have.
- Senior staff often suffer the most from lack of being greeted.

Holding the door open

Endless fire doors in offices have created a manners crisis unique to the workplace. 'What do you do,' Matt asks, 'when there's a whole series of doors and the person ahead of you keeps holding them open for you? Do you thank them the first time or the last or every time?' People often thank effusively when the first door is opened for them but become increasingly morose and sullen, giving the impression to the person trying to be polite that they are nothing but a nuisance.

- Thank the *first time* the door is held open.
- Thereafter, smile sweetly.
- Don't giggle or get fed up. Would you rather have the door slammed in your face?

At the urinal

This one is for men only. In women's toilets, we hear, it's chatty and unhierarchical. Although in a comprehensive school where I once taught, the deputy head was often criticised for peeing too briskly. But in the office gents, as in all public men's toilets, silence reigns. From time to time there is a drive to institute the 'working piss' but it always comes to nothing. If all those lined up at the urinal are of equal status, it's straightforward – don't talk. Trauma only sets in when senior management are suddenly present. 'What's worse,' somebody said, 'seeing your boss's willy or your father's?' Of course some pushy types, far from being disturbed, might see a chance to push.

- Don't start promoting yourself at the urinal.
- If, on entering, you find the boss in the toilets, get adept, like Matt, at reversing straight out again.
- Or you can go in the cubicles, but leave the door ajar to avoid suspicion.

In the lift

Lifts usually impose a complete suspension of normal life. Going up and going down, people become non-people, even mothers and children no longer know each other; everybody stares at the walls. Lifts in offices are different. Here there might be opportunities to hobnob with top people (didn't Melanie Griffith get her big break in *Working Girl* when she encountered Harrison Ford in the lift?). Matt once heard 'some whippersnapper trying to discuss the quarterly results with the MD in an embarrassingly familiar way' and on another occasion 'two women from accounts, which is my department, talking at the tops of their voices about the postboy's sex life or what they imagined it to be'.

- Don't corner senior management in the lift to try and make an impression. It's not fair on them. There'll be other chances.
- Senior management, when in the lift, should always make a point of condescending to speak.
- Don't forget that the other people in the lift can hear what you're saying.
- Don't talk shop in the lift. It's boring for everybody else.

In the canteen

An extraordinary lunch-time embarrassment – perhaps unique – occurred not in the canteen but in the gardens of Soho Square in London. A young woman was enjoying a picnic with a friend. She was suddenly aware that her boss, Mr Noy, was nearby, apparently trying to pick up a young man. He hadn't seen her. Ideally, she would have liked to move away. But this wasn't possible because Mr Noy was *so* near that he might have overheard even a whispered explanation or seen her should she have got to her feet.

Her only hope was to try to remain concealed behind her companion. As she was tiny this was not such a challenge. But she soon found that she was not quite tiny enough and every time her companion moved, she had to move too.

In Matt's canteen, which they call a restaurant, it's not quite as bad as this. But he often sees people with their trays in severe uncertainty about *who to sit with*. 'Supposing it's an editorial assistant from one of our magazines like *Seals and Sealants*. There's space on my table. Maybe he's thinking, "I don't want to sit with him, he's a boring money man." Or perhaps it's, "All the people on that table are more senior; I can't sit with them." '

Other piquant dilemmas: do you sit at the already over-crowded table with your friends or join the new person who is sitting on their own? If it were a social occasion, you might make an effort. But this is work, isn't it? And there's the getting-away problem, because, unlike at normal meals, you often have to leave someone to finish their lunch on their own.

- Don't sit with the management if there is space elsewhere. It'll look like crawling.
- If the only seat left is at a table occupied by management, they should put themselves out to offer it to you.
- As on ordinary social occasions, don't leave people on their own. Just because you're at work, it doesn't mean you've turned barbaric.
- If you have appointments, calls to make etc. it can't be helped if you have to leave someone to finish their lunch

alone. But you should say, 'Excuse me. Sorry to leave you on your own.'

Distractions

One of the pleasures of office life is that there can be dropping in, against which there is elsewhere a taboo (see **Dropping in**, page 83). Someone might drop in from legal for a natter or you might yourself pop over to finance for the same purpose. Dropping in or by creates a distraction which is usually most welcome, even, if the truth be told, to the miserable sods too busy to say hello in the corridor and those eaten up with ambition. But occasionally there is work to do. Zoe, who is at that stage of being enthusiastic about her job in PR, building up contacts in the press and so on, says, 'If I have to listen to one more gargantuan discussion about Annie's matching handbag for her wedding or what sort of towels they're putting on their wedding list . . .'

- Don't distract people if they are busy.

Interruptions

People interrupt at work for much the same reasons as they do in social life – because they've got something far more interesting to say, ideally about themselves. Sad to say, Zoe is something of an interrupter, often forging into the managing director's office regardless to talk about *her* concerns or triumphs. 'Some people seem to think it's part of being thrusting and successful – just barge into your office and start telling you how wonderful they are,' says Matt. Or they just want you to think about their problem or help them with some difficulty they've got. They never think that you might be preoccupied with something. They cause havoc; the interrupted don't know whether they're coming or going. There are a lot of them about.

- Always ask if it is convenient to speak, even if the person is kindly operating what is called an 'open-door policy'.
- If someone is clearly busy, go away and come back later, even if their office door is open.

Thanking

She doesn't exactly say so, but Zoe probably thinks, 'Why should I have to thank? It's her job.' But her managing director has taken rather a lot of trouble with Zoe, helping and encouraging. A little appreciation wouldn't come amiss. We hear a great deal about the sad state of the self-esteem of the majority of the human race. Besides, nobody likes a thankless job. Matt complains of being caught in the middle. 'My work's OK. I think the bosses just forget to say thank you. The younger ones, you help them out because they don't know the first thing about acquisitions or loss adjustment, and you don't get any thanks for that either.'

- There can never be too much thanking in the workplace.
- It isn't *only* senior staff who should thank.

Presents and cards

In *Green Wing*, Channel 4's crazy 'hospital' comedy, a gloomy figure trudged round the administrator's office. 'Do you want to sign Karen's leaving card?' Everybody complied and, as the bearer of the card was sloping away, a voice was heard to enquire, 'Who's Karen?'

Outside the workplace, correspondence is neglected (that terrible backlog of thank-yous etc., on the necessity of which see **Thank-you letters and cards for meals and parties – a major rethink**, page 214), but in the office little enthusiastic messages are written on cards for unknown people every day. There is an obsessive mania for cards and presents for every conceivable anniversary and would-be special occasion. Vast amounts of time are devoted to buying them, getting the cards signed (a huge administrative undertaking), raising money for presents (another massive job), as well as buying and wrapping them. One woman I spoke to was amazed to receive a card signed by the entire office because she was going to the christening of her second cousin's child, the second cousin being someone she hardly knew.

'People come round with these cards at least once a week. Someone's mum hasn't been too well, someone's getting married, having a baby, moving house, getting engaged,' says Matt. 'I always sign them, even if I don't really know who they are. But I wonder how people have got the time for all this.' Zoe, careful with her meagre salary, resents the expense. 'Somebody comes up to you and says, "We're all putting a tenner in for Aimee's present. Is that OK?" You can't say no, can you?' Others, less popular (said to have smelly feet, not to share their chocolates), are lucky to get a tenner spent on their entire present.

Another phenomenon is excessive sending of thank-you cards (although there might be a general lack of thanks in the same workplace – see **Thanking**, page 38). 'Our MD's PA was too busy to get the flowers for the reception desk once,' says Zoe, 'and I volunteered since I was going past the shop in my lunch hour. I got a card for that.'

- It makes sense to sign a card for someone you don't know when that person is leaving – maybe, unknown to you, they cleaned a sticky patch off the photocopier which would otherwise have ruined your immaculate document.

You are thanking them for their contribution, whatever it might have been.

· Otherwise, departments or smaller teams might give cards on significant occasions (not just when they feel like it). If this custom is established, everybody must be included (no nasty favouritism) and trouble must be taken to find out when and to whom they might be sent.

· Although 'rules' about the giving of presents might seem clinical and mean-spirited, the alternative is that popular people are showered with all kinds of largesse while others get very little, and younger employees resent having to fork out while expectations from receivers of gifts rocket through the ceiling. One person told me she was outraged only to get an M & S breadboard after working in a place for six months.

· A leaving present should be a token of appreciation, not a measure of worth.

· If 'thank-you cards' are over-used, they lose their meaning. In the workplace, they should be reserved for some quite exceptional favour or kindness.

· A card signed by everyone is not right for a bereavement. Don't ask why; it just isn't.

Smelly food – the CupaSoup nightmare

Eating in the workplace and eating on the street (see **Munch as you go and What's that smell?**, page 15) can upset in the same way, only the former is worse because certain sights and smells are harder to escape indoors. In an office, people being known to each other, it could be that loathing of what someone is eating is really loathing of them. But actually some food is unbearable just by itself, Batchelors CupaSoup being the shining example. Zoe says, 'Rice cakes! Ugh! Why do adults have to eat baby food?' At least she can stay in the room with them but when a male colleague tucks into his daily takeaway, she has to hide in the toilets. 'One MD's office I knew smelt so bad nobody could stand to go in,' says Matt. 'The business nearly collapsed because nobody was telling the guy anything. It turned out he liked cheese and he used to keep some weird stinky French stuff in there.'

- Many workplaces have rules about eating at your desk. Where there are none, avoid smelly food. Watch out for your colleagues crinkling their noses.
- Food that might be all right elsewhere won't really do in the workplace – fish and chips, burgers, Indian or Chinese

takeaway. It's the smell. It just doesn't go with the nice clean office smells of computers, paper and rubber plants. Also, it's all very well when a whole group is chomping through a takeaway, but one person gnashing away on their own isn't an attractive sight.

Office parties

With the rising tide of money in recent years there have been more and more office parties. Employers think they are providing a treat. Employees do nothing but grumble. 'Have we got to go?' 'I'm not sitting next to her.' 'Only sparkling white this year! Cutting back, are we?' One year Matt was required to organise the Christmas party. He nearly died. It had to be an elaborate event with a theme and a band and entertainment and a seating plan. Nothing else would do. Afterwards, everybody was invited to fill out a questionnaire criticising it to their heart's content.

'But research shows,' says Matt, 'that if we just gave them vouchers, they wouldn't feel valued.'

You can't win.

The anarchy and drunkenness of office parties are legendary. But the inexperienced should be wary. It's not what it seems.

The classic horror scenario is the younger employees behaving just as they would at their own party, *only worse*. Telling the boss what they really think of him or her is just the beginning. They will insist on strip poker; if met with general recalcitrance they will take all their clothes off just to make a point and sit on the lap of the most spinsterly of the PAs. This is a prelude to being violently sick and collapsing on the floor.

Senior staff may not behave much better. I heard of one boss who, in his speech, took the opportunity to tell his workforce that they were a useless lot who would be lucky to find their jobs waiting for them when they returned after New Year. Another, who had cleverly seen to it that only very gorgeous young men were employed in the media-planning department, took the opportunity of the Christmas party to snog them all.

If not out of control, you might, like Matt, have trouble thinking of something to say. 'One year I spent the time discussing how we could reduce paper costs with a colleague.' This is very bad – talking shop. But suddenly having to wean yourself off this kind of thing and talk to people you think you know well in a different way is disconcerting.

- Anarchy at office parties is far more controlled than it appears.
- You can get drunk but you should not be incapable.
- Don't be sick.
- Don't make an exhibition of yourself.
- Don't talk shop.
- In some cases you need to talk to people as if you've never met them before (see **Getting to know people: Perfect questions**, page 145).
- Sex, on the whole, is a mistake.

[44]

- Drugs should not be taken, unless actually provided by the boss.

Leave it as you found it and Would you do that at home?

At school, teachers always say to the litter bug, 'Would you do that at home?' Usually the answer's, 'Yes, there's somebody to pick up litter.' They mean their mothers. In the workplace the attitude is similar. 'I'm too grand to tidy/clear away/remove rubbish. The "cleaners" will do it.'

But watch out – perhaps it isn't the cleaners who are doing it. Zoe turned the meeting room at her PR agency upside down. She was overexcited. She was leading a little strategy meeting for the first time. She wanted a non-hierarchical arrangement of furniture. *But did she put it back how it should have been when she had finished?* Guess who was in there next? And who had to put it all back again? That's right. The managing director. Who snagged her Nicole Farhi skirt in the process.

In Matt's office, the bugbear is the coffee area. It's a horrible sight: ring marks everywhere, drips and splashes, coffee powder scattered, unattractive brown lumps in the sugar. Not even cats could get it into this state. 'Every day someone puts the jug back on the hotplate with just a little bit of coffee left. After a while it evaporates, leaving a sticky mess which is hard to clean. Once or twice the jug's got stuck to the hotplate and we've had to buy a new machine.'

Just because you're in the office, it doesn't mean you haven't got to:

- Tidy as you go.
- Leave it as you found it.

Is that your mug?

Once again, the workplace wields its mysterious power. Normally upright citizens turn into serial petty criminals at work. 'I get through one mug a month minimum,' says Matt. Luckily he's not one of those office workers who get attached to their mug. But where do they go? Only rarely is there an explanation. A newly arrived boss I know of once threw away a whole cupboard of old, cracked mugs only to find that they were the jealously guarded personal mugs of his new staff. The thief is rarely caught in full possession. In the mug racket they're shifted on sharpish. In offices where newspapers or magazines are provided, these can be guaranteed to have evaporated by midday. Otherwise it's pens. 'You've got a lot of pens,' somebody said to Zoe one day. She had indeed and most of them weren't hers. Everyone in an office either has so many pens they don't know what to do or none at all.

• If it's not yours, don't take it.

Taking advantage

Zoe, still rather green in the PR world, got a call the other day from an out-of-town journalist on a trade paper of some kind. He was coming up to London. Could she recommend a restaurant, perhaps one near her office? Her answer was simple: no, she couldn't. Other times she has had calls asking about hotels or enquiring if it's possible to 'buy' any of the T-shirts her agency were giving away last summer. It was no again to the hotel and as for the T-shirts, they were £15 each. Her managing director, when she got to hear about this, was at first annoyed but eventually rather admiring. 'Good for you,' she said.

Zoe hadn't really got it. These people were looking for freebies. Matt can tell of similar grasping ways. 'We've had suppliers demanding to be taken to particular restaurants, then, when they get there, commandeering the wine list and ordering expensive wine. Sometimes they cancel at the last minute or take calls all the way through lunch.'

It's not just clients who behave like this. Junior employees, when taken out by their head of department or equivalent for a welcoming lunch, are often astonishingly quick to order. This is because it doesn't take very long to find the most expensive thing on the menu, that being the only object. Ideally, it should be twice as expensive as anything else. Senior managers are helpless to stop this practice, but they do call perpetrators 'lobsters' after the item they're most likely to choose. Luckily, Zoe behaved well at her lunch with the managing director. She doesn't like lobster or really even know what it is.

Customers are at it too. 'You've miscalculated my phone bill by 12p. I want twenty minutes of free calls and a sequined draught excluder.' Or, in the supermarket, 'My trolley's wonky. I want a year's supply of frozen peas.' They call it compensation but actually it's something for nothing.

- Stand up to vulgar grasping clients and customers. They know they're just trying it on. They won't dare to protest if you refuse to give in to their outrageous demands. They'll crawl away, utterly crushed.
- Don't be a lobster.

Overdoing it in various ways

Who is loathed in the office beyond endurance? Is it the hellish monster of ambition, the insatiable nosy parker or the self-important, full-time martyr?

Stories of unbelievable behaviour abound. A senior colleague of Matt's was sacked. His deputy visited the fallen man at home at eleven o'clock at night, apparently to commiserate but really to discuss a strategy for getting the now vacant post. A similar thing happened in publishing when a redoubtable editor (the job was her life) was made redundant. A colleague was so sorry, how appalling, how unfair etc. and what about so-and-so, the famous crime writer, I really think I'm very well placed to take him on now, don't you?

This kind of thing is the equivalent of turning up at your gran's the minute she's dead, the corpse not cold, and taking possession of the electric blanket from under her.

Others strut about the workplace, saying, 'My most outstanding quality is my raw intelligence,' 'I feel I make a huge contribution with my sense of humour,' 'I'm definitely ready to take on this challenge.' Zoe tends in this direction at times but can be forgiven on account of her youth. Once she announced that in ten years' time she saw herself 'heading up' her own company. Conspicuous use of jargon is another feature of the ambitious, and this can often be happily combined with putting down colleagues: 'He needs to focus on his presentation strategy if he wants to be taken seriously,' 'She's just not tuned in to the synergistic approach,' 'He's going nowhere while his Powerpoint skills are stuck at that level.'

These types spend most of their time plotting and scheming on their own behalf. They leave actual work to others, which is where the martyr, who might also be ambitious, comes in. 'Yes, I was working,' bellowed Mrs Thatcher at three in the morning as she emerged from the Brighton Grand after the bomb. Martyrs are always talking about weekends, about how they don't have them, they're too busy working. They sit in corners in offices with their heads down, a massive force field of disapproval slamming out at anyone who might be talking about what they're going to have for lunch or whether they might buy a new pair of shoes. 'You can't be in a fit state for work if you've been out until three in the morning,' they say if they get the chance. Martyrs dislike competition.

'I had 368 e-mails when I got back from holiday.'

'You were lucky to get a holiday. I only managed to snatch a weekend on the Isle of Wight and when I got back from that I had 873 e-mails.'

'It took me the whole day to deal with them.'

'I know. I was up all night with mine.'

Unambitious martyrs are always ill and always telling their colleagues that they look ill. 'The way they work us in this place it isn't surprising. We're all falling to pieces. I've had this cold for six weeks . . .'

Finally, a disturbing office trait that might be displayed by martyrs, the hellishly ambitious or the insufferably smug. The director of finance for whom Matt works can be relied upon to say, at least twice a day, 'As director of finance, I do feel that . . .' 'As director of finance, I was surprised that the auditor didn't speak to me first . . .' 'As director of finance, I feel I should be sitting next to the group chairman . . .' 'I'm telling you, as director of finance, this is how I want it done . . .' It's called Pulling Rank.

- If you're ambitious you should keep quiet about it.
- Boasting of all kinds provokes nothing but ridicule and contempt.
- Martyrs are black holes; they get everybody down.
- Martyrs spoil the fun.
- Don't pull rank. We live in a democracy.

Mobile phones at work

Recently, Matt suffered an embarrassment. 'I was getting a fair number of calls in a meeting. First of all, the boss asked me to switch my phone off and everybody cheered. Then afterwards he said he wanted a quiet word: "I don't know why you even have it out on the table. We all know you've got one." He said I looked like a wanker.'

Maybe this was not quite the way to put it. But the boss was right.

The mobile phones of really senior professionals (not quite Matt, yet at least) are never seen or heard. Tim Hely Hutchinson, who is in charge of a gigantic publishing conglomerate, possesses a mobile phone but as his secretary will tell you, 'it won't be switched on.'

Which is just as it should be. People like that can't be at everybody's beck and call.

Lesser employees in open-plan offices drive their colleagues round the bend if they take personal calls on their mobiles every ten minutes, especially if, like Zoe, you have the cicada ring tone.

So, it's perfectly simply really:

- Only allow mobile calls to interrupt other business (i.e. meetings, discussions, however informal) if you want to appear desperate and disorganised as well as rude.
- Remember the old-fashioned virtue: one thing at a time.
- If you know that you will have to take an urgent call in a meeting (even a meeting with only one other person), issue a prior warning and ask to be excused. If that isn't possible, say, 'Excuse me, would you mind if I take this call.' Then disappear.
- Keep apologising.
- If your mobile is for personal use, it should be switched to silent mode in an open-plan office.

Office e-mail

Big groan from Matt. 'I get hundreds and hundreds of e-mails a day. Half of them go, "I've mislaid my copy of *The Rough Guide to Romania*. Has anybody seen it?" or, "Has anybody's cat littered recently? I can offer a super cat-friendly home for a cute kitten." The other half are all great long screeds about editorial changes on *Dumper Truck Today* which are nothing to do with me.' Then there are the e-mails from his immediate boss, the director of finance, some of which aren't very nice. 'I think he sits in his office getting more and more worked up and then he just can't help himself, he fires off a really poisonous e-mail. Usually he's got totally the wrong end of the stick.'

In Zoe's office, the managing director makes a point of talking to people, especially if there's something she wants them to do. But Zoe is always e-mailing her, despite sitting five yards away. Ten minutes later she'll say, 'Did you get my e-mail?' and start explaining what it says, which seems to make the poor woman rather tight-lipped.

E-mail promotes carelessness. Too much information, too many ill-thought-out suggestions are being hurled about. Some of them fall into the wrong hands, leading to the tragic downfall of politicians such as David Blunkett or government spin doctors such as Jo Moore who wrote the infamous 9/11 e-mail. Matt knows of someone who got an e-mail from head office which said, 'Perhaps your relocation expenses could be included in your redundancy package.' This was the first this person had heard of redundancy. Prior warning gave him an advantage in the ensuing negotiations. Research has shown that British offices have the highest incidence in the world of sending sensitive e-mails to the wrong person.

Sometimes, the topmost figures in the office are the most out of touch with the etiquette arising from technological developments. Matt and his colleagues are perturbed by their managing director's habit of starting e-mails, 'Dear so-and-so,' and signing off, 'Yours sincerely,' as you do in letters. They wonder how to reply.

Some businesses and organisations that invite the public to e-mail them are slow and inept in replying. Say that you e-mail because you can't get some feature of their website to work. Their reply, if and when it comes, might be 80 per cent general spiel about the wretched website, its aims and intentions, even its history, and only 20 per cent cursory and incomprehensible reference to your actual problem.

- Don't e-mail everybody.
- Don't use e-mail to keep people at a distance.
- E-mail can result in too much communication of the wrong kind. Be careful what you say and who you send it to.
- Managers may sit in their offices and fume about the incompetence of their underlings but firing off intemperate e-mails to these people is not a good idea. Usually, managers end up looking foolish when they do this.
- Within the office, don't nag about e-mails or, worse still, start telling someone what the e-mail you've sent them says. If you've chosen to communicate by e-mail, then do that.
- As with private e-mails, there is no need to start 'Dear . . .' An e-mail is the equivalent of the memos that were once the standard form of written communication within offices. Who it is from and to, and the subject, are given at the top.

- But e-mails should be courteously signed. Not, 'Yours sincerely,' or 'Yours faithfully,' (these are for letters) but, 'Best wishes,' or 'Thanks,' as appropriate.
- The whole point of e-mail is speed. If someone wanted to trundle a letter through the post they'd do that. It mucks up the whole thing if you take ages to reply. Acknowledge all e-mails on receipt, even if a full response has to wait. One small publisher of a hotel guide (which presumably values feedback from readers) caused outrage by grandly announcing that it aimed to reply to e-mails *within six weeks*. This is perfectly useless.
- If businesses invite e-mails from customers and clients it is essential that these are dealt with by people who can read and write. Often they are not. Don't be surprised if people are enraged by the discourtesy of having half their questions ignored and the other half misunderstood.

Condoling at work

'A few years back,' says Matt, 'my rich friend at work was away for about ten days because his father died. When he came back I kept trying to find an opportunity to say something to him. But there was always somebody else about and I felt so awkward about it anyway. It was a bit of a nightmare. I became obsessed with it.'

Oh, dear! This story is all too familiar.

What is better? This kind of excessive delicacy or Zoe, meaning well, saying rather too loudly, 'Sorry to hear about your dad,' before telling the person that she's read in a magazine that it takes four years to get over a major bereavement.

Or a third approach – which is to do nothing at all?

- Condolences must be offered. Not to do so is extraordinarily cold and unsupportive, especially since a bereaved person is likely to need support just to do their job, at least initially.
- But if you all flock round the stricken person the minute they come through the door, they might be overwhelmed. Bereaved people often say they don't want 'fuss'. 'Fuss' seems to be demanding a response from them. It's the last thing they want. For this reason, some people, sadly, insist on keeping their bereavements private.
- So, it's best if you can speak to the person quietly, when nobody else is around. If you don't know them very well, you only need to say, 'I'm sorry to hear about . . .' It's their choice if they wish to say more.
- If no such opportunity arises, or it does but you are too embarrassed to seize it and hope pathetically for another, then there's a very simple solution: SEND THEM A CARD OR WRITE A BRIEF LETTER. If, after one week, you have failed to convey your condolences, this is what you should do.

Communications Manners

'Don't take that call!' Mobile phones in social life

Less than ten years ago, everybody was getting home after work to a stubbornly unyielding answerphone, a reproachfully not-winking red light. 'Nobody ever calls.' No matter how many times we said it, it never made any difference.

And now, everywhere you look – on trains, on buses, in shopping centres, in restaurants, at wedding receptions – what a miracle! What a transformation! So many happy people talking away into their mobile phones.

Connected at last!

You can be sure that Zoe will be one of them, in a bar with her girlfriends, all of them texting away, taking and making calls – running their own telephone exchange, really.

'Without my mobile, I'd literally be dead,' Zoe says.

But . . . but . . . one moment, please. There's something lurking. Matt sits in the driving seat of the family people carrier while his wife, Lucy, conducts her social life on her mobile phone beside him.

Come along, Matt, why don't you admit it? You feel like the chauffeur, don't you? It's taken you years to realise it, but you resent it, don't you? There was a time when it was new, it was glamorous – all this calling, slashing through everything.

But it isn't any more.

We can see it for what it is now. It's antisocial.

It's time to take a stand.

- On all social occasions, from just a meeting of two friends to a wedding, mobile phones are the enemy. They mean people are not joining in, they're imposing, they're disrupting, they're pursuing their own agenda. It would have been better if they'd brought some DIY with them or a book, which they could get on with quietly in a corner. SWITCH THEM OFF. People like Zoe just can't understand this. She was on the phone for ten minutes the other day. The friend she was with dared to complain. Zoe told her to 'chill out'. How selfish can you get!
- Mobile phones have made us anxious. Liberate yourself. Leave it alone. The missed call won't be someone saying your house has burnt down. If you just can't wean yourself, 'check' your phone out of sight of the others, in the toilets perhaps. Remember the old days. In Mrs Gibbs's youth telephones were kept in draughty hallways and only used, for reasons of economy, for the briefest of conversations. 'If that's Mrs Oxshott, I hope you're ringing to apologise.' This was her mother's style of answering the telephone.

- It's perfectly obvious – but how often does it happen? – if you really *have to* either make or receive an urgent call during a social occasion, you should explain the situation to the others at the outset. When the time comes, *remove yourself from the scene to deal with the call.*
- Whatever you do, keep apologising.

An appeal to the good, too-silent majority: Don't put up with it. Don't suffer in silence. If you come across someone like Zoe, especially if you are an older person, use your seniority to clobber them. Don't hesitate to interrupt offensive mobile-phone users mid-call, ask them to move away, to switch off. If they are passengers in your car, stop, pitch them out, especially if it's raining. Be like Lindsay Duncan in Stephen Poliakoff's TV play, *Shooting the Past*. 'Don't take that call,' she boomed at a miserable little person who was reaching for his phone, about to interrupt her imperious flow.

For telephone manner see **On the phone**, page 71.

Switched on or not switched on? The responsibilities of ownership

This might seem contradictory. There are plenty of times when mobile phones should be switched off, out of sight, gagged etc. We don't want them being lobbed like grenades into social life. In a recent TV drama a clueless teenager took a call on her mobile at a wedding, *during the speeches*. But, on the other hand, there are quite a lot of people who possess a mobile phone but rarely answer calls and take days to respond to messages. Is this just a tiny bit confusing for those trying to get in touch?

You could say that Zoe is perfectly behaved in returning calls and answering messages. On the mobile, which she is for most of the time, she is sociable. But not everybody would want to be quite so available.

Matt, who is a whizz with his mobile phone at work, tends to the other extreme in his private life. He is often switched off and can take days to respond to messages from friends. This will not do. Zoe and I both assume, if a call or text has not been acknowledged within the hour for no apparent reason, that the person must be lying mangled by the roadside.

Does it have to be like this?

- Being reasonably available on your mobile phone doesn't mean you're going to turn into a mobile-phone junkie or suffer total loss of privacy. Owning a mobile phone implies that you want to get in touch with people quickly, so it's only fair that it should work the other way round.
- Make sure your phone is switched on at crucial times – if you are meeting someone in a public place or anywhere away from home, for example.
- In some situations, being switched on is a matter of life and death – as when I got separated from my friends in a labyrinthine car park in Italy in 37 degrees of heat. NOT ONE SINGLE ONE OF THEM had their phone switched on. I can tell you, I've never forgotten it.

- Swiftness is the whole point of a mobile phone. If people are prepared to wait a few days for you to find the time for a leisurely chat they'll ring your land-line. RESPOND TO MESSAGES QUICKLY. Hours rather than days.
- If you're fantastically busy, you can always send a text message. Or make calls (legally) while driving.

Texting and non-texting

The texting revolution has been one of the glories of modern life and if you won't join in (like Matt) you're a miserable spoilsport. Some people, mostly non-youths, shall we say, absolutely dig their heels in and refuse to text. This is such a shame. The delirious popularity of this means of communication is only partly explained by its convenience, sociability and cheapness. Of course, it's most helpful to have the latest on *Big Brother* or *I'm a Celebrity* flashed to you wherever you are in the world. But the real charm is the bogus significance given to banal banter by its means of conveyance. So it is essential that text messages are entirely pointless.

- Don't be stuffy.
- If you don't know how to text, do please learn. Don't be a text refuser.

Text conversations/ending text conversations

It's mealy-mouthed not to engage in a bit of bouncing back and forth if you get a text message that seems to invite it. Text 'conversations' should not be dull like party small talk – the weather is never mentioned. The sillier the better.

You might get a message: 'Catastrophe: tissue in wash. Bits everywhere.'

You reply: 'Oh, no. Heart bleeds. Deepest symp.'
Them: 'Can't believe it. Thought I'd checked all pockets. Feel utterly let down.'
You: 'How about a nice cup of tea and a sit-down?'
Them: 'Would love to but can't see an end to these bits.'
You: 'Maybe easier to deal with when dry?'
Them: 'Sure you're right. But can't stand the sight of them.'

Now, at this point you might just begin to feel that this conversation could come to a useful end. This is where Matt gets in a state (although to be honest his text conversations are about football and usually take place during matches).

But it's not that difficult. Just remember one thing. It doesn't matter what you say as long as you don't just fall silent. That is a snub. In Matt's case, he could say, 'Text again after match?' or 'Got something in the oven' (unlikely, especially in a football stadium). Any effort to end the text flurry considerately will be appreciated – or ought to be.

Tone/Misunderstandings in text conversations

Zoe once got a text from one of her girlfriends which said, 'Terrible car crash last night. It's all over with Ed.' This friend had been having a difficult on–off relationship with Ed for some months. 'I thought it meant there'd been a real car crash. I thought he was dead. But it turned out she meant there'd been a car crash of *emotions*.' Another time she'd had a row with a friend who suggested reconciliation at the cinema. Zoe didn't think this the ideal venue. 'Not sure about cinema,' she texted, which created the impression that she didn't want to make up at all.

- The telegraphese of texting can give rise to misunderstanding. Don't attempt to say anything too complicated in a text message.
- DO NOT USE ONLY CAPITALS IN A TEXT MESSAGE: IT LOOKS AS THOUGH YOU'RE SHOUTING.

When not to text

Sometimes texting can be a substitute for communication, not a form of it. It *can* be discourteous, evasive and even cowardly to text.

- The worst example of this is ending a relationship with a text message. We'll just have to hope that Zoe has never stooped this low. She's certainly not admitting to anything. It's a shame that some form of public humiliation cannot be arranged for perpetrators.
- Matt and his wife were most put out when someone they didn't know very well thanked for hospitality by text (see **Thank-you letters and cards for meals and parties – a major rethink**, page 214). 'Thanx 4 din' was a bit abrupt, Matt thought. Don't thank by text unless you know the person very well.
- In a similar vein, it is impersonal to invite someone you only know slightly by text.
- Nor should you break bad news or send information that might be in any way distressing to the recipient by text. It is far too abrupt and there is no opportunity for any further comfort and support that might be needed. A number of companies have been rightly vilified for sacking people by text.
- Some people try to conduct rows by text. The golden rule is IF YOU CAN'T BRING YOURSELF TO SAY IT TO THEIR FACE, DON'T SAY IT AT ALL. The medium itself, as with e-mail (see **E-mailing**, page 65), can promote

intemperate behaviour. Zoe's friend, now ex-friend, Jenni became addicted to sending nasty messages. ' "You haven't even got a car!" "You're just jealous because I can afford the Maldives." She'd think of something horrible and send it off straight away. She was totally out of control.'

Language and grammar in texting

The other day Mrs Penelope Penney, headmistress of the Haberdashers' Aske's School for Girls, sent a text message to a member of her staff. 'Thanx 4 yr message' it said.

- There we have it. Text language is open to all. Don't listen to Zoe who thinks it should be reserved for the young alone. But you don't *have* to use it.
- If you use text language, make sure you don't turn illiterate. Exam candidates have been known to write, 'Microbes R fnd in the intestine.' It shouldn't be like this. Just because you learn Spanish, it doesn't mean your English goes down the drain. This is the age of the multi-skilled. Just add text language to your already extensive collection of skills.

E-mailing

E-mail is a highly desirable form of instant communication, whose liberating effects are yet to be fully embraced and whose darker side is yet to be fully understood.

'Can you really do thank-yous by e-mail?' asks Matt. Yes,

of course you can. In fact, it is preferable for thank-yous (see **Thank-you letters and cards for meals and parties – a major rethink**, page 214). The only form of social exchange it is not suitable for is letters of condolence. Don't listen to fuddy-duddies who insist that sending an e-mail isn't taking enough trouble with your thanks. This is the nonsensical masochistic approach to manners, perhaps to life in general, which dictates that true gratitude must involve suffering and painful sacrifice, in this case all the palaver of writing paper, envelopes, stamps and post boxes. If you feel guilty about your e-mail thanks, why not spend some time sticking drawing pins into yourself in penance?

'What about spelling and grammar?' Matt again. Let's deal with his difficulties before getting on to the real horrors. Where did this idea come from that e-mails can be written in gibberish? Many centuries have been devoted to the development of a system of grammar, punctuation and spelling. Why throw it all away now? All e-mails should be properly spelt and punctuated. Even if you exist in an office culture, as Matt does, where this is not done, your efforts will be appreciated. Let's be bold and speak the truth. Illiterate is illiterate. It means it can't be understood. Abandon the struggle to make sense of the preschool outpourings of your friends and colleagues. What we need is a literacy filter, equivalent to the device that detects viruses.

- Yes, you can thank by e-mail.
- Literate e-mails are much less likely to lead to disastrous misunderstandings than illiterate ones.

- Don't be fooled. It only *appears* to be a contradiction that crazy abbreviations and phonetic spellings are permitted in text language. This is mostly out of necessity and because texts are shorter (see **Language and grammar in texting**, page 65).
- Recipients of e-mails sometimes take umbrage if the message does not open with, 'Dear . . .' like a letter. But an e-mail is not a letter. It is the equivalent of a note or postcard. It does not begin, 'Dear . . .'.
- But senders of e-mails should always sign off in a friendly or courteous way, either 'Best wishes,' 'Thanks,' 'Love,' or, if you must, 'Luv,' – unless, that is, you wish to create a malicious effect. It is not enough just to put your name. This is abrupt.
- Group e-mails are dangerous. If it's an invitation, recipients will cast a critical eye over the other would-be guests. And the surprise is spoiled. Generally, there might be resentment at being lumped in with others. Technically, it is possible to conceal that you are sending a group e-mail. Find out how to do this.

Now on to more drastic aspects. This instant medium provokes thoughtlessness and carelessness. It is not often recognised that successful e-mailing requires proficiency in reading and writing. It's not something just anybody can do. Many people with a university education are deficient. If somebody e-mails, 'Are you free next Thursday? I'm just back from Africa. I don't want to see another crocodile,' the chances are the first part of the message will be overlooked.

So: no reply to question = sender offended. Or if the message says, 'She fainted dead away,' you can be sure the rumours of 'her' death will be flying around within seconds. Equally, if you reply to the question 'Are you meeting at 7.30?' with 'Yes, we're meeting at 7.00,' the recipient can be forgiven for misreading 7.30 for 7.00. The writer appears to be confirming their misapprehension about when they are meeting. If the answer to a question is no, then why not say so?

- So, take a long, hard look at yourself. If you suspect that your abilities in reading and writing are at all deficient, it would be a kindness to refrain from e-mailing until they have improved.

But there are worse carelessnesses than this. Many people find that, within weeks of acquiring e-mail, they have fallen out with all their friends. They wonder why.

- It may be that they're not on the ball about replying. If you don't reply promptly to e-mails, don't be surprised if your friends, snubbed and enraged, come crashing through your window in person. The whole point of e-mail is that it is quick, quick, quick. It is ruinous if you take more than twenty-four hours to reply. What's your excuse? All you have to do is click on 'Reply'. You might have been asked a question you can't immediately answer, in which case you can send a quick e-mail explaining this.
- Some people announce an e-mail address, so all their

friends send them a friendly welcoming message, 'Welcome to e-mail. Welcome to the twenty-first century. It will transform your life,' and so on.

And then – nothing.

Eventually, when pressed, the person says, 'Oh, I never look at my e-mail.'

What is the point? Nobody would say, 'Oh, I never open my letters. I never answer the telephone.' If you don't want e-mail, don't have it. Having it and not using it is making a nuisance of yourself.

- Being a spoilsport about chatting is another way to get on the wrong side of people. A little flurry of e-mails, the more pointless the better, is a very pleasant way of passing the time. 'Hi, how are you?' 'Good. And you?' 'Think I'll get some shirts in to soak this evening.' 'Interesting, what are you using?' and so on.

- But some people are dismal and won't play. Now, it may be a little awkward to extract yourself from a session of chat whose drive and purpose is on the wane (and you may need to get on with other important work) but there are gracious ways of doing this (see **Text conversations/ Ending text conversations**, page 62). And this difficulty is no reason to be po-faced and refuse to join in from the start.

- Or it may be that the nightmare e-mailer does at least reply, but abruptly. 'Can't do that.' 'Not a good idea.' 'Dunno.' 'Yes.' 'No.' In speaking, 'yes' can sound enthusiastic, gentle, sympathetic etc. but in writing, unadorned, it will sound like 'yes'. Short phrases and words should be handled with care in e-mailing. Don't be in too much of a hurry. Make sure your tone can't be misunderstood. Sometimes it's worth spending a few extra nano-seconds adding some lovely softening verbal wadding.

But there is worse, something that causes all these other wrongdoings to shrivel to nothing, and this is the e-mailer who has lost their head, who sends psychotic messages full of random loathing. Something about the medium induces this condition. In the old days, less-than-pleasant letters might have been written but never posted. But now someone seized by sudden fury only has to sit down, slam out some bile, press 'Send' and off it goes. It's all over before they know it.

So it is that cyberspace is crackling with vile correspondence.

'I've had some unbelievable e-mails,' says Zoe. You wonder why. 'One said I was a fat bitch – just because I couldn't go to her party. I'm sure people wouldn't write stuff like this in a letter, let alone say it to my face. What was really weird was that when I saw this person again it was like she'd never said it.'

- Senders of these horrible e-mails never think that the recipient might be at work or in some other less-than-ideal situation in which to receive a knock-out blow. I hesitate to ask the victims to forgive the perpetrators who don't know what they are doing.
- Why can't those who feel themselves beginning to fill up

with poison act before it is too late? Write the hateful e-mail. That might make you feel better. But put it in the 'Drafts' box for at least an hour and then delete it. Otherwise, just keep away from the e-mail. Keep your fingers busy with something else.

Sexy e-mails – see **Filth**, page 190.

On the phone

- A businesslike style, announcing yourself with, 'Hel-lo,' or even, 'Hel-loo,' (massive emphasis on the first syllable), ending with, 'bye-ee' and saying, 'Yip,' a lot in between is now often mistaken for a good telephone manner.

  But we've had enough of this clichéd nonsense. It is most unfriendly. Even Matt has acquired this ghastly habit of saying, 'Hel -lo.' He has to drop it at once. It's not him at all. There's nothing wrong with, 'Hello.'
- It's not necessary, indeed not advisable, to give your name when answering. You don't know who might be calling. There's no need to give the number either. It's rather like giving directions. Nobody listens. Nobody has the first idea what number they've dialled. Don't bother. Just say, 'Hello.'
- It's up to the caller to ask, if they don't already know, whether they are speaking to the right person. They should also announce themselves. 'Hello, it's . . .' or, 'Hi, it's . . .' Don't say, 'It's . . . speaking,' unless you particularly want to appear old-fashioned.

- When you are using a land-line, it is more than likely that the wrong person will answer – the wife, the mother, the husband, the child. If these people are known to you at all, you should engage in a bit of light banter with them. 'I can never think of anything to say,' Matt complains. Well, you just have to. The trick is to drive that weary, going-through-the-motions undercurrent from your voice. Answerers sometimes cut off the banter by saying, 'You want to speak to Britney? I'll just get her.' This doesn't help.

- The land-line nowadays is used for extended conversations in the comfort of the home (although less so in the case of the under-thirties). But there is still the difficulty, even between close friends, of ending the call. Ending calls, saying goodbye, moving on at parties, ending e-mail and text-message exchanges – there is a national complex about this. 'Anyway,' followed by a sigh and silence, is usually a sign that the telephone conversation is beginning to expire. Nevertheless, it will crawl on for quite a few more minutes before one or other of the telephoners says, 'I'd better let you go now,' or, 'I mustn't keep you.'

  These euphemisms are distasteful. Everybody knows they mean, 'Why don't you bugger off?' Russell Harty used to terminate telephone conversations with 'I've had enough now,' which is at least honest. Why not be straightforward but friendly? 'I'd love to go on talking but that chicken will be ready by now.' Or 'I've got to get on with the children's packed lunches for tomorrow.' Usually there is a good reason why you have to finish the call. Just say what it is.

If we sat around chatting all day we'd never get anywhere.

- Of course, for some these attempts at termination are a cue to start off on a whole new story. There are certain people (make sure you're not one of them) who are famous for going on and on when they're on the telephone. In real life, these people go on too, but to a lesser extent. Mrs Gibbs knows quite a few of them. 'What I do now,' she says, 'is just put down the receiver, cut off the call. It's so simple. Sometimes they ring back in a frightful panic. "I thought something had happened to you." So I say, "I'm quite all right. It was lovely talking to you. Thank you for calling. Goodbye." But usually they don't. I suppose they just go jabbering on and never realise there's nobody there.'

- Some land-line calls never end, but others require an effort to sustain. It is very difficult to make a brief land-line call nowadays. Gone is the time when people shouted at each other down the telephone in draughty hallways and it was a race to see who could slam the receiver down first. Now there is an unspoken expectation that a land-line call will last a minimum of two minutes. For brief exchanges of information, text messaging, e-mail or mobile phones are used. So if you *are* using a land-line to reply to an invitation or some other short purpose, some further friendly chat is called for. Try not to be half-hearted about this. It can be fun.

- It isn't necessary to return land-line calls as promptly as you should mobile calls, text messages or e-mails. If a friend leaves a message on your land-line, you can assume they are hoping for a proper, long natter. They will be prepared to wait a day or two for you to find the opportunity.

Leaving messages

Long-winded messages left on land-line and mobile answering services are much disliked. Some people seem unable to tolerate the lack of response and say everything over and over again in the hope that the wall of silence might be beaten down.

- Get on with it! If you find yourself saying, 'As I say . . .' something's wrong. Don't um and ah. Don't leave long pauses.
- Alternatively, don't be too snappy, too impersonal, too businesslike.
- Worst of all are the people who leave their number too fast. There's this lightning cascade, all terribly slick and impressive, but really it could be anything. You might have been listening to a nurse expertly whipping off a plaster. PLEASE SPEAK SLOWLY. Somebody's got to write that number down. How can they if it whizzes by at a hundred miles an hour?

Matt once had to ring his answering service six times before he could catch a number in its entirety. Then, when he dialled the hard-won number, he was greeted by the lady saying, 'The number you have dialled has not been recognised.' He had to start again.

It's cruel to do that to a person.

Let's Get Together: Inviting and Accepting Manners

A question of honour: Being stood up, 'flaking' and the commitment problem

It might seem odd to start at the end, as it were, with social events not happening, friends not meeting. But it is, in fact, the beginning.

Young people call it 'flaking', the call at the last minute: 'Sorry, not really in the mood. A bit knackered. Can we do it some other time?' In this way, a date to meet up with a friend for the evening might be cancelled. For a bigger occasion, such as a party, there might be no call at all. Zoe Miller is a terrific flaker. The more she makes a song and dance about how fantastic your party's going to be, she's going to wear such-and-such a dress, she can't wait etc., the more you can be certain she won't turn up. It's no use trying to talk to her about it. She's barely conscious of what she's doing. But it's something she does.

In Mrs Gibbs's day they were called 'scratchers'. 'It was

supposed to be disgraceful behaviour but some people got away with murder.' It's not just a modern phenomenon. Matt, sadly, finds himself on the receiving end. 'At my wife Lucy's fortieth there were two no-shows and two people who called up to cancel *after the party had started* – bloody mobile phones! Their excuse was pathetic, too.' He is uncharacteristically incensed. 'The seating plan went out of the window. And it cost us money.' And sometimes his mates stand him up when they're supposed to be having a 'boys' night out'. 'That's a bugger because Lucy and I almost have to pass an act of Parliament for me to get a night out on my own – the babysitting, you know.'

Jacking in, not turning up – is it worse now than ever before? It doesn't really matter. It goes on. And it strikes at the root of everything. Friendship, less intimate relation-ships, social life, cannot get off the ground, cannot even begin if there's no agreement that people are actually going to show up when they said they would. So, if you are a victim of unreliability, you're entitled to feel aggrieved. Don't take it lying down. Make a fuss.

A friend cries off an evening out at the last minute:

- If their house has burnt down, or every pipe has burst or they are actually dead, they have a reasonable excuse.
- If they've got into some terrible tangle with work (although usually it's possible to foresee such things and give warning when the date is made) and this has never happened before, you can forgive them.
- In very extreme circumstances and if it's a very close

friend, you *might* let them off at very short notice if they get an absolutely fabulous once-in-a-lifetime offer (dinner with Madonna, Posh and Becks and Sir Elton) and they are so apologetic they are barely recognisable.

· If they give no less than four days' notice, you might be tolerant of them having another offer which they'll have to miss (i.e. invitation to dinner, Robbie Williams concert tickets, or invitation from Mrs Onassis, as happened to Cecil Beaton) whereas your date could be rearranged. But they must approach with the utmost diplomacy and tact. And never have done this before.

If someone hasn't turned up to your party and they said they would, in other words they actually accepted the invitation, fight back. They mustn't be allowed to get away with sowing discord where there should be harmony. You have been generous in offering hospitality. What a way to respond!

· A list of no-showers conspicuously displayed at the party will act as a warning to others – rather like those admonitory dead crows farmers hang round the edges of fields. Stop at nothing to ensure that no-showers are named and shamed and others are warned off them.

· Or why not – for the no-shower is often a wretched guilty creature who'll be phoning up the next morning wanting you to make them feel better – for once, cast off the shallow mask of manners and call a spade a spade.

Here's why no-showers are ghastly:

- No-showers make all kinds of low excuses. 'It's a big drinks party, I won't be missed.' Well, let's hope that they're right about that and that by the time of the next party they've been forgotten about altogether. OF COURSE YOU'LL BE MISSED, YOU FOOL. WHY DO YOU THINK YOU WERE ASKED IN THE FIRST PLACE?
- And why did they say they'd go?
- Sometimes they whine, 'But I don't really know the hosts. They won't mind.' Once again, hideously missing the point – they've been asked because the hosts want to know them better.
- No-showers think, I don't dare to actually refuse the invitation. Something better *might not turn up*. I'll say I'll go but really I'm hedging my bets.

There are occasionally genuine reasons for cancellation, last-minute or otherwise. Still, it is worth pointing out that some people manage to get through their whole lives without once cancelling. Mrs Gibbs has so far managed eighty-five cancellation-free years. The first Lady Curzon, Vicerene of India at the turn of the nineteenth century, was so sickly she had to be carried into state banquets where she would manage a teaspoonful of brandy, before being carried back to her carriage in time for a complete collapse.

Let that be an example to us all!

- If you cancel claiming illness, you should be unable to stand up. Illnesses should not come on at the last minute. Joanna Lumley couldn't come to the novelist Anthony Powell's 80th birthday lunch because she had flu, but her message only arrived at 12.55. (Flu is anyway a very unsatisfactory excuse. Very few people actually have flu. They just mean a cold. This is not to suggest, of course, that Miss Lumley didn't have flu.)
- Some givers of the 'pressure of work' excuse, harking back to the eighties, still offer it with a self-important flourish as if hosts being ditched will be impressed rather than annoyed. But nowadays we hear more about 'work/ life balance'. If this is your explanation, you've got it wrong. Very, very occasionally the work excuse is viable. But it's still your fault for being disorganised. Gales of apology are called for.

Saying no nicely

A casual suggestion to meet up, a more elaborate invitation – old friends or even lovers can fall out if these are abruptly dismissed.

The curt response is too often heard: 'Not free, then. Sorry,' or 'No. Can't do that.' This will always seem like a more fundamental rejection than is perhaps intended.

- You should always explain *why* you can't go. Some people claim that under old etiquette it was 'correct' to offer no explanation. In fact, etiquette books from the thirties and forties specifically state that you *should* do so. Anyway, it is obviously unfriendly and barrier-slamming to be secretive about your plans. If you do it to people you don't know very well they will feel snubbed and won't ask you again.

- An invitation, even if refused, should be thanked for:
  even if you didn't particularly want to go.
  even if you don't like the person inviting you.
  even if you are in fact available but are refusing anyway out of loathing.

Divorce etiquette

There's a lot to be said for going back to the old days when divorce meant instant sacking from social life or, at best, severe demotion to small country towns where the separate parties might make pallid attempts to start again.

Now there's all the agonising that goes on amongst the friends of the divorced, trying to be nice to both parties, trying not to take sides! Matt and his wife, Lucy, writhed for days, when planning her fortieth birthday, over whether to invite both halves of various divorced couples, only one half or no halves at all.

Why bother? It's not your fault they got divorced. Why should you have to suffer for it?

- Do exactly what you want.
- If you really do like both of them equally (which would seem unlikely), then invite them both, should the need

arise. You can tell them that this is what you've done, and they can fight it out amongst themselves if necessary.

- But the truth, which you're being too polite and nice to admit, is that one of them was always much more your friend, you never really liked the other one and it's a big relief to see the back of them.

- Or, the divorce was entirely the fault of just one of them (ideally, the one you never really liked), who has behaved so atrociously that he or she deserves to be ostracised. Therefore, speaking your mind (in this case by pointedly not inviting) is more than a duty; it is a pleasure.

They keep inviting us but we don't want to go

It's like a huge underground mass of weevils gnawing at the roots of social life. There's so much of this going on. People don't like to admit, even to themselves, the real reason for refusal – *they just don't want to go*. Why is this?

Matt has never known the feeling. 'I always think, nice of them to ask. It could be fun.' Zoe, on the other hand, is often mysteriously unenthusiastic about proffered hospitality. She has a knack of discouraging inviters. We've all known someone like Zoe – someone who seems to be *digging their heels in*. Yes, there are definitely a lot of them about.

Why are they so secretive? Could it be that there's something just a little shameful about not wanting to go? Is it just a little mean-spirited, a little unadventurous? Could the motives be low? We won't get on because they're richer than us, too old, too suburban?

- Don't expect much sympathy if you just don't want to go.
- You're lucky to be asked at all. How do you know you won't get on, until you've been?
- Is 'getting on' the point? Aren't you interested in people, even people who may be quite different from you? Where's your spirit of adventure?
- Who knows – if you accept the invitation, maybe they'll decide they don't like you either. At least, then, you won't have to go again.

Dropping in

Quentin Crisp said that when the English say, 'Do drop in,' they mean goodbye. People continue to say, 'Do drop in,' but nobody ever does. Somewhere there must be a yearning for dropping in.

In the old days, middle- and upper-class people had a system for dropping in. It was called 'calling' and there were all kinds of quite sensible rules that prevented embarrassment. Very grand houses in London turned themselves into sort of restaurants on certain days of the week and people known to the family could drop in and get an entire lunch.

It all sounds so sociable and friendly.

Nowadays, we've turned starchy about it. Matt would never drop in. It would kill him. But Zoe does and so does

Mrs Gibbs – but they only drop in on people of their own age.

Let's not be so difficult. Let's have more dropping in.

- The mobile phone is the great sword of hope for the dropping-in movement. If you're in the neighbourhood, phone them up, see if they're at home. Don't turn up without warning – that really would be dangerous. They might be having sex.
- Don't take offence if they say now's not the best time – unless they are abrupt and seem alarmed/outraged and generally anti-dropping in.
- If someone offers to drop in, be pleased. But don't feel obliged – that ghastly British disease. If it's really not possible, you can say so. You could even be bold and suggest an alternative definite date.
- Near to mealtimes is probably not ideal for dropping in. But if you drop in at twelve o'clock and they say, 'Please stay for lunch,' don't assume that they just feel obliged. If you want their lunch, say yes. If their offer was only polite, it'll teach them.
- Attempts to drop in fail most frequently because no one is home. Don't be discouraged. Keep on trying. Expect only a 10 per cent success rate.
- Don't be discouraged, either, by the negative portrayal of droppers-in on TV and radio. In *Dynasty*, for reasons never explained, the lift shot straight up into the middle of Joan Collins's 'lounge area', delivering all manner of menacing unannounced guests, including hired assassins.

Linda Snell in *The Archers* only calls round to deliver reprimands, perhaps for having untidy fields, or to bully the unsuspecting into being in a mystery play.

Written invitations: What to write?

People do worry so. When you look at the barbed-wire tangle of choices it's not hard to see why. Matt Lawson and his wife Lucy agonised for an entire week over the invitations to her fortieth birthday, which was to be a fabulous re-mortgaging affair (sit-down dinner in a restaurant, band and so on). Would 'requests the pleasure of your company' be too formal? How about 'Hey! Let's celebrate'? – the informal approach – but would that be naff? 'Eventually I convinced myself it didn't really matter,' says Matt. So, what did they end up with? 'Oh, it was terrible.' He looks sheepish. Well, what? 'I really can't remember.' There is a silence. 'It was something like, "Lucy's going to be forty (Gasp!!! Horror!!!) Help! . . . Help! . . . Please come to a party, otherwise she might not survive . . ."'

A lot of people will sympathise with poor old Matt.

For Zoe Miller, still sparkling in her twenties, the invitation must be whacky: 'Zoe Miller presents The Christmas Party. Sparkling wine or you're dead,' is a typical summons to a bring-a-bottle party at her flat share in Balham. Computer graphics, scanned-in photographs and slightly illicit use of the office photocopier are also involved.

'What is "A Party!!!!"?' Mrs Gibbs asks. She received such an invitation from her great-nieces. 'There were a lot of unflattering old snaps of my niece around the edge. It took me ages to work out it was an invitation at all. It may have been more stuffy in the old days, but at least you knew where you were. It was either "At Home" or "Requests the Pleasure". That was it. The former was more informal and you wrote on the card exactly what it was: dinner, lunch, drinks etc. The latter was for weddings and very grand dinners with tiaras and medals (quite out of our class, I'm afraid).'

Let's sort out all this muddle:

- Under thirties: Beware of printed cards and generally appearing stuck up. 'Requests the Pleasure' and 'At Home' are out of the question. You'll come to them later. Go for self-designed invitations, the crazier the better. If you want people to bring specific drink, put 'Sparkling white wine, if you can,' rather than, as I once saw, 'If you've no objection, please bring Beaujolais' (sounds as if you're about to consult lawyers). Zoe's gunpoint demand for sparkling white is not a good idea either.

- Over thirties: Invitations like Matt's, that seem to cajole rather than invite, just sound desperate. Attempts at wit and jollity often fall flat but a quietly dignified invitation can never be wrong. The time-honoured 'requests the pleasure of your company', for fairly large occasions, is hard to improve on. It is truly courteous, both humble and warm, if you stop to think what it means. Don't bother with pointless variations such as 'would like the pleasure of your company' or 'take pleasure in requesting your company'. 'You are invited . . .' is too abrupt. 'So-and-So would like to invite you . . .' has a feeling of the New English Bible – plain and boring.

- At Home cards are making a comeback, perhaps because they are useful when you do not want to go to the expense of a specially produced card. You can also scrawl little personal notes on them.

- Since you will only have written invitations for a special or large occasion it is worth doing it properly. If it's to be a bit of A4 paper photocopied at the office you might as well not bother. Card should be of a decent thickness and any photographs or artwork clearly reproduced. If in doubt as to size, go for postcard size invitations.

Inviting by telephone or e-mail

Most inviting is done by telephone. Which isn't so easily done. Quite a few people get nervous or embarrassed, and start to crave e-mail. Matt says, 'Sometimes I've dialled the number and the phone's ringing and I'm suddenly thinking, Why would these people want to come to dinner with us? What a cheek!' Others suddenly find themselves speaking 'refayned': 'Will you dayne with us . . . ?' Or launching into long and desperate accounts of the virtues of the other guests as if to compensate for the obvious wretchedness of the hosts.

- It is vital to speak in person when inviting. Avoid answering machines. People won't be terribly thrilled at the prospect of spending time with you if, in the process of inviting, you appear unwilling to talk to them.
- You should invite only friends by e-mail and very close friends by text message (see **When not to text**, page 64 and **E-mailing**, page 65). But beware of a classic modern mix-up about dates and times if you use these means. I once missed a terribly expensive charity dinner because I e-mailed the host, 'Is it 31st November?' He replied, 'Yes, it's 30th October,' which I misread as a yes to my idea of the non-existent 31st November.
- As with written invitations, a straightforward and dignified approach is best. 'Would you like to come to dinner . . . ?' 'We'd love you to come on . . .'
- Don't mention the other guests; this can sound desperate

(as if you alone are not good enough) or suggests that you are fielding a cast of 'characters', making the occasion feel artificial before it has begun.

• Matt Lawson worries about whether to have some 'chit-chat' before or after the invitation is issued. Afterwards is best, unless you want to give a furtive impression (see **On the phone**, page 71).

What is being offered/how to explain/what words to use

It is vital to be clear, but people often aren't. Will there be food? This is the question that often rages after invitations have been issued nowadays. Zoe Miller was once invited by an older colleague to 'come round for the evening'. Only when she got there did she find that there was to be dinner, quite an elaborate one, in fact. The trouble was, feeling hungry after work, she'd had a curry and a bar of chocolate. 'It was a complete nightmare. I just about managed to force down the second dinner. The worst thing was, the hostess was really into food and cooking so we had to talk about it all the time as well.'

• Hosts are responsible for explaining exactly what they are offering. It is embarrassing for guests to ask.

Everybody knows what 'dinner' or 'buffet' on an invitation means. The difficulty arises with 'drinks' or indeed the general term 'party'. Matt recently received an invitation from a senior colleague for 'drinks' at twelve o'clock on a Sunday. 'Everyone was sniffing round the office trying to find out if we'd get lunch or not. A lot of us were coming from a distance so we just had to hope we wouldn't get turfed out after an hour and a half with nothing to eat.'

As it happened they didn't.

The other anxiety is what to call the kind of food you might offer at a drinks party. I was once, bizarrely, on the phone to a hostess from her own party (she was held up in Munich on business). I said, 'You're giving a marvellous party. We're having nibbles.' She said starchily, 'What do you mean by "nibbles"?' Matt thinks 'nibbles' or 'drinks and things' are naff expressions, but the alternative 'canapés' is stuck-up. Be too specific and you might put some people off. 'If it says "mulled wine", I won't go,' says Mrs Gibbs. 'I'd rather have cough medicine.'

What a tangled web! Here's a ground-breaking solution:

- 'Drinks' on invitations should mean food (either 'nibbles' or 'canapés' or 'things') in quantities varying according to the time given. This is a new rule, so pay careful attention. For 'drinks' at eight o'clock on a Saturday there should be sufficient 'finger food' to get guests through the evening, although not as much as a full dinner. A shorter 'drinks' party, say between 6.30 and 8.30 (often a 'work do' – a leaving party, celebration, book launch etc.) will involve less food, but still a fairly substantial 'nibble'. Just crisps and olives is disappointing. The only exception is a private view in an art gallery where there is never anything to eat and the wine is always filthy (see **What shall I give them? Food for others**, page 116).

When to invite

Before the war, sending out invitations, even for weddings, more than three weeks in advance would have seemed absurdly pretentious and self-important. Today we all like to advertise 'how booked up' we are and the ludicrous idea has taken hold that it's an insult to invite anyone less than about two years in advance. (Matt was asked at Christmas-time to a dinner in March. When it came round, he was poisoned by a piece of cold mackerel cooked in tea.) But Ivy Compton-Burnett, when asked what she most valued in a friend, replied bluntly, 'Availability.' We seem to have forgotten that.

It's an awful state of affairs.

And, do you know, it's *not* true. People aren't booked up. I once lived opposite some semi-celebrities and *they were home all the time*. It's worst at Christmas, when everyone makes a great parade of their invitations. But a friend of mine once gave a last-minute party and a vast number of people, some of them *quite well known,* were astonishingly available.

So we can be quite clear:

- a week to ten days in advance is quite enough for dinners and perhaps a month to six weeks for larger parties.
- If you want to snub someone who invites you to a New

Year's Party in June, you can say you've got a funeral on that day.

But what about more seriously last-minute invitations – less than two days beforehand? We probably shouldn't go as far as the hostesses in Evelyn Waugh's *A Handful of Dust*, who always invited John Beaver at the last minute, 'occasionally even later, when he had already begun to eat a solitary meal from a tray ... "John, darling, there's been a muddle and Sonia has arrived without Reggie. Could you be an angel and help me out? Only be quick, because we're going in now."'

This is a bit much.

But why not be realistic – and rational? Social occasions evolve in haphazard ways: some people can't come; the mix of guests begins to veer from your original plan; you suddenly can't think why you didn't think of so-and-so beforehand.

- Let's not be too stuffy about last-minute invitations – both giving and receiving them.

Who to invite?

Some hosts believe that the success of a smaller party, especially a dinner, is in the inviting. This is certainly true if you ensure that you have the right balance of shy to outgoing guests and enough people who can be relied on to take an interest in others. But less so if you try to match people according to personality, interests etc.

'Sometimes you think, They're both in finance, they'll get on OK,' Matt says. 'But it's always a disaster. They start competing or one wants a favour off the other.'

'I was once invited to meet someone because we had Bournemouth in common,' says Mrs Gibbs. 'But she'd only been there for a week on a cake-decorating course and had awful weather. So there was nothing doing there.'

• Avoid inviting to larger parties shy and retiring people who would know nobody but you: you'll be too busy to spend the whole evening with them and the misery of seeing them standing alone in the corner could be ghastly.

Confirming

In the Lawson household there's often a crisis ten minutes before the start of a dinner party. 'What if none of them turn up? Maybe we didn't tell them the right date? Maybe they've all forgotten?' Some hosts will phone the guests the day before to confirm. They say something like, 'I'm just ringing to confirm you for tomorrow.' 'Yes, we've thought of that,' says Matt, 'but it'll make us seem like fusspots, won't it, or socially insecure or something?'

This is true.

It would be better if *guests* were to ring to confirm the day before. At the moment they tend to call at 6.30, when your thrashing in the kitchen is at its height, to ask what time they should arrive or whether the dinner's still on.

- Come along, guests! Let's see you ringing to confirm dinner invitations the day before and stop making a nuisance of yourselves.

How to reply

- A written reply sent through the post is only necessary for a wedding invitation. Otherwise you can reply by phone or e-mail to any kind of invitation.
- Never reply to an invitation in the third person, e.g. 'Lord Aardvark is pleased to accept . . .' This is very old-fashioned and indeed wrong, even if the invitation is itself written in the third person (which it only is out of necessity).

No reply at all!

Failure to reply to invitations *at all* is probably one of the most prominent social diseases of our times. Absolutely everybody who has ever issued invitations of any kind complains of it. 'I've got some statistics, actually,' says Matt. I won't bore you with the details, but they're horrendous. Even venerable persons like Mrs Gibbs suffer. 'I invited some neighbours for a drink. They didn't reply. I was most put out. Also, I didn't like to go out in the street in case they were there. Then, lo and behold, on the *day* I'd mentioned, they phone up: Oh, yes, we'd love to come, how kind and so on. I didn't quite have the nerve to tell them it was too late, but my mother would have done, I can tell you.'

- Please, if you are serious about improving the world we live in, REPLY TO YOUR INVITATIONS PROMPTLY.
- Your reply should be a straightforward yes or no. Only say, 'I hope I'll be free,' or 'I'll hope to make it,' if you want to inconvenience as well as insult your hosts.
- Hosts should display prominently a list of non-repliers. Over the mantelpiece is best. This is particularly effective since non-repliers often turn up anyway.

Disinviting

Disinviting may be the glorious culmination of a row, in which case manners are not the issue. But some people think they can get away with it when invitations have been extended perhaps as a favour to a friend or to somebody's visitors (in other words to people they don't know very well or at all). They can't.

Asking to be invited. Can I bring a friend?

Another worry is: Can I bring someone? Do I dare to ask? There is both too much of this going on and not enough.

In theory, at least, what can be the harm? It is the essence of social life, bringing people together. Apart from anything else, at a large party it is the unknown quantities who create a frenzy of excitement rather than the dear familiar faces.

Nor is this the sloppy modern behaviour it might at first seem. In the old days, you could write a letter of introduction for one of your friends, introducing them to another. Recipients of these letters were obliged to offer hospitality to that person, which frequently meant asking them to a party *without the mutual friend even being there.*

- Nevertheless, guests should approach with caution and sensitivity. Too often they don't. A well-known collector of eighteenth-century French textiles is quite capable of asking to bring *five or more* extra people – a kind of entourage. This is not welcome. One person (or two if a couple) is the absolute maximum. There has to be a special reason for proposing someone. Most often it is that they have unexpectedly come to stay on a visit from abroad, more rarely you think that the hosts would especially like to meet them. It should certainly *not* be merely for your own convenience or entertainment.
- Don't make a habit of it, either. If all guests got it into their heads that they could drag in a few hangers-on, hosts would be at their wits' end and quite a few guest-stuffed houses might fall down.
- You should not suggest further guests if they're going to cost a lot of money. Matt Lawson was put out when somebody asked to bring his sister to Lucy's fortieth. 'Didn't he realise we were paying 75 quid a head?'
- Hosts should not be prickly. Who knows, new blood may

be just what your party needs. But if someone is just taking advantage, tell them so (in the nicest possible way, of course).

- Hosts should have a firm grasp of who the extra people are. A friend of Matt's swore blind that she'd spoken at length with Hugh Fearnley-Whittingstall at a party of his. Matt doesn't know Hugh Fearnley-Whittingstall, he doesn't think he knows anybody who knows him. But maybe, just maybe he was there. Could it be that somebody asked to bring him and Matt wasn't paying attention? Now he'll never know.

- Asking to bring someone to dinner, as you might want to do if a friend has come to stay with you unexpectedly, is a more serious matter. The procedure here is baroque. Phone and explain the situation; offer to drop out. The hosts can then extend the invitation to the other person, but they certainly don't have to. Or they might say that they have run out of space and/or money and suggest that you might prefer to come to dinner another time. You can then either accept this proposal or say that you will come alone as originally planned.

- Extra guests are completely out of the question at weddings.

Not invited!

Sometimes, the whole point of the party is that certain people haven't been invited. Some people make a habit of this. It is nasty. More usually, hosts are just thoughtless or mean-spirited. If you invite one person from a particular group, what about the others? If you're thinking, 'Have I got to have them?' perhaps party giving isn't really your calling.

- Include, be generous. Don't get a reputation for stuffiness. If you suddenly remember someone as the last minute approaches, don't be stuffy about that either (see **When to Invite**, page 91). Invite them.
- Make a list of people likely to hear of the party from those you *have* invited. Then consider just how snubbed these unfortunates are going to feel. If you think they might be severely cast down, invite them.
- If you are one of the uninvited, wait until the occasion has taken place before making a small scene. 'I hear you had a fabulous party.' 'How did your party go?' Let them know you've noticed. Make them just a little uncomfortable.

A lot of people, usually men, find themselves shut out from weddings. Matt was distressed 'when one of my best mates, at least that's what I thought he was, didn't invite me to his wedding. He said it was just going to be very small. But actually it wasn't that small.' The real reason, of course, was pathetic anxiety that Matt and various other mates of the groom wouldn't behave well enough. This is the usual reason.

- If you are a victim of discrimination of this type, don't take it lying down. Things will not be the same again. Have the bridal pair realised this? It may be a kindness at least to ask.

Clothes Manners

What to wear?

In about 1932, Lady Astor's daughter was seen walking in Bond Street *without a hat on*. The witness to the crime was Mrs Gibbs's mother, who happened to be an acquaintance of the formidable Lady Astor. 'My mother agonised for days,' Mrs Gibbs recalls. 'Should she inform on the wretched girl or would that be too cruel?'

Now it's heady freedom: bare midriffs, pierced tummy buttons and visible thongs and underpants – and that's just for school. In 2003, Jamie Oliver even saw fit to go to Buckingham Palace without a tie.

Are we happy? No, of course not. It's worry, worry, worry. 'I'm just not sure whether jeans are OK. Should I wear a jacket?' Matt moans. If the truth were told, he's more worried about being the odd one out than giving offence. According to Annalisa Barbieri, who at one time was a fashion 'agony aunt' for the *Independent on Sunday*, most of the people who wrote to her were preoccupied with conformity: 'Can I get away with wearing this? ... Will it be acceptable if I wear that ... ?'

But haven't Matt and all these other people noticed:

- At ordinary social occasions you can wear what you like – jeans, trainers, T-shirts or suits and ties. There are no rules. Rejoice and wear your clothes, whatever they are, with conviction. They should look *intended,* which means, incidentally, not dog-eared, grubby or what you slept in.
- If you've really got no idea, you only need remember two things: don't be scruffy (*see above*) and avoid at all costs that strained, trussed-up look of someone who has hauled themselves into their Sunday best.

- If you have to, you can always undress (within reason). Take off your tie, hat, jacket if you insist on feeling out of place. Even your tiara is removable, as the Duchess of

Devonshire discovered on a recent visit to Windsor, where not even the Queen was wearing one. So the Duchess took hers off and put it on a chair. She said that Windsor Castle was the only place where you could leave your tiara on a chair and be sure of finding it later.

- If you are the victim of a spillage or a spattering at a party, you should not feel that you have been disgraced. Do not try to conceal the marks but rather wear them as the honourable scars of battle.

But what about weddings, certain kinds of work 'do', some private parties where those phrases, 'Black Tie', 'Morning Dress' or 'Lounge Suit' appear on the invitation? Zoe, who has her fair share of weddings and, in the PR world, grand awards ceremonies where 'black tie' might be in the offing, doesn't think twice. She knows exactly what to wear – hat or no hat, skirts, trousers, dresses. She knows what's smart. So does Mrs Gibbs. 'I'm never wearing a hat for a wedding again as long as I live. The last one I went to, my friend Bunty Scott-Fox's hat fell down the loo – just where it belonged, although it was a perfectly nice hat.'

No, it's the men who have to be told what to wear. When Matt and Lucy were asked to Glyndebourne (he was bored to death; football is his thing), he was straight round to the hire shop for a dinner jacket. If it looks like a smart evening outing – usually to do with work – it's on with the suit and tie.

Oh, the dreary conformity of it all!

- Don't put 'Black Tie' or 'Morning Dress' on your invitations. It's rude. Also, your wedding or grand reception won't be any grander because the men were rigged out in cheap-looking, ill-fitting hired garments.
- Don't bother with 'Lounge Suit' either, even though it's what the Blairs do at Downing Street. What is a lounge suit? Does anybody know? Did anyone ever know?
- If there are discriminatory dress codes on invitations, ignore them. They are ill mannered. You know how to dress.
- If you venture into a public place where the sinister Black Tie mafia might still be at large, such as Glyndebourne or the rival country-house operas – resist them. There's nothing they can do about you anyway. Revel in their ill-mannered disapproving looks.

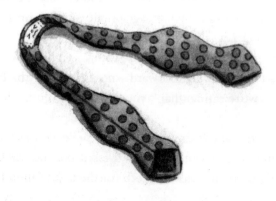

- Men, if you feel that you *must* wear a tie, this is the cue not to. We've got to get away from this pomposity about ties – any old tie, no matter what state it is in. And the same goes for the accompanying suit – it can be grubby, ill fitting or not very nice, but it's a suit and tie so it's smart. Follow the pioneering example of Tom Ford, David Beckham and Ewan McGregor, who have been superbly glamorous at weddings and other top-notch occasions without ties.

- In hotels and restaurants, if they try to make you wear a tie or complain about your dress, leave immediately – after an argument.

Matt wonders if, when he is staying in a villa with friends, he can go to lunch without his shirt on. Of course, if his pecs are magnificent (as no doubt they are), he would probably be welcome naked.

But this isn't quite the point. We can't have one rule for Adonises and another for the less aesthetically pleasing. It isn't fair. Besides, can the saggy, hairy, spotty horrors be relied upon not to start flaunting themselves?

- No, it's quite straightforward – no unnecessary bare flesh when we're eating, thank you.

A final word about dress: people can be 'correctly' dressed but still atrocious. Or 'wrongly' dressed but nice. Just how much offence can pieces of cloth (or the lack of them) give?

Greetings Manners

The social-kissing question

'Far too much kissing,' says Mrs Gibbs.

Did it start in the seventies with gay men defiantly greeting each other in public with elaborate kissing rituals? Now it has penetrated far, even into circles formerly renowned for their rectitude. A headmistress of a top girls' school was seen recently welcoming a former member of staff with a double social kiss.

But, typically, there is uncertainty. How many times? What to do with the hands? Do straight men kiss their gay friends? What are the alternatives? What about shaking hands? Is social kissing established practice in all areas of the country?

'In my day you shook hands. Kissing was for actressy women,' Mrs Gibbs explains. 'Lord knows how all this non-sensical carry-on of today would have gone down.' This is a point of view.

- Respect for seniority is vital. When greeting older people, wait to see what they do. 'People just bear down on you. I suppose if I had a poker or a broom handle I could beat them off but it wouldn't be very friendly, would it?' If Mrs Gibbs, at eighty-five, wishes to shake your hand and say, 'How do you do?' (to which you reply, 'How do you do?'), then that is what should happen.
- Beware if you're out of your own stamping ground. Matt once got caught out trying to kiss a whole roomful of dour Scottish matrons. 'I think they thought I was a sex pest. It was one of the most embarrassing experiences of my life.' As above, if you're not on home ground, wait and see what the people of the place do.
- If you are in or around a big city and the age group is twenty to fifty-five you are likely to be in social-kissing territory. You say hi or hello on first meeting. Don't shake hands (people under thirty are puzzled by the handshake and giggle uncontrollably at the proffered hand). After that you get on to social-kissing terms with sluttish speed – usually at the end of the first meeting unless it has been very brief.

The question remains: 'How do you actually do it?' Matt complains, 'Lucy's always telling me I'm rubbish. The trouble is, if you let them give you one and then you try to give them one but they've decided to give you another and you've got quite a big nose like me, you can get a bit of a collision. But if you just let them kiss you twice, you get it in the neck for being inhibited and patronising –

or at least I do. Also, I'm never sure what to do with my hands.'

- Two kisses are quite enough. Four is just too theatrical – we are British, after all! It should be one kiss each, so whoever goes first, waits for the other to kiss them. While kissing, you should hold lightly on to one another at either the elbow or the forearm.
- Great comfort for Matt – you don't have to be good at it! Indeed, you mustn't be good at it. Awkwardness and embarrassment are essential in British life if you don't want to be thought 'cocky' or 'slick'.
- Whether you're compelled to practise social kissing or whether you launch into it by design, you've got to actually kiss. Air kissing, especially if accompanied by ear-splitting MWAH-MWAHs, is just annoying.

Who kisses whom? There's no great mystery here, but what happens when a straight man and a gay man coincide? Matt was once kissed by a gay man at the end of a dinner party. 'I didn't mind, honest, except that some of the women were smirking because they knew it had never happened before. But I wouldn't be so sure what to do if I met that guy again.'

- Gay men shouldn't go around forcing a lot of helpless straight men to kiss them.
- Straight men shouldn't make a silly fuss when kissed by accident, as it were.

Do straight men need help? Their greetings and farewells usually consist of aborted handshakes, awkward back-slapping and clumsy grabbing of arms, if anything at all. You might suppose there's room for a bit of tidying up but I think not. There's a certain charm to it all. Let's leave them as they are.

- Straight men don't kiss each other, at least not yet.

Right on Time: Clock Manners

Sorry! We're running late

Up and down the country, people are late. They're meeting their friends, they're going to a party, they're going to dinner at someone's home. They're late.

Zoe will be one of them. 'Oh, yes,' she says, 'I'm often a bit late, I suppose.' What does she mean by 'a bit'? She doesn't really know. That's part of the point. She's not going to get all anal about the time. But if you want to know, she's usually forty minutes late. 'Has anyone ever complained?' There's not much point in asking. Of course they haven't. Zoe's look implies that nobody would be so uncool, so unchilled out. Matt is cagey on the subject. Yes, people are late. It's a bit of a problem . . . He peters out. He's reluctant to talk.

Only Mrs Gibbs is robust: 'I went to a little supper party. A woman was terribly late. We had to wait and wait. When eventually she arrived, I thought at least there must have been some kind of catastrophe but not a bit of it. She'd been doing her nails or some such. I wasn't at all impressed. But I could see the other guests thought I was a finickety old thing.'

In the old days, if you were late the meal started without you. People who had servants were even afraid of being late for dinner in their own homes. Mrs Gibbs knew some people in the fifties and sixties who 'never dared to eat in anyone else's house because their cook would take offence. You could invite them for a drink at 6.30 but they would sit on the edge of their chairs desperately eyeing the clock, terrified that they'd be late back for Mrs Little.'

Perhaps this is why, today, we make such a show of not caring about lateness. Our guests must be happy. We must never disapprove of anything they do, we must never make them feel on edge. So what do we say when they're forty-five minutes late? Come on, admit it! 'It doesn't matter.' Of course! 'It doesn't matter.' 'Don't worry about it.'

So it's hardly surprising that people are getting later and later, if it doesn't matter. But it's time we grasped the nettle by the stalk. It does matter. Latecomers are a nightmare. We hate them.

We hate waiting in the street or some other uncomfortable public place for our late friend. If we're at home cooking, we think, Haven't *they* ever tried to cook anything? Don't they know you can't just put food in the oven and *leave it there*? Matt begins to open up. 'I suppose it's true. There's a bit of a meltdown in the kitchen if someone is late.' Sensitive sorts, like Matt, think 'that they didn't much want to come in the first place.' (Now we're really getting somewhere with him.) Latecomers make everything else late. Food maybe doesn't appear until ten o'clock. The other guests are drunk and only thinking that now they won't be in bed until one and they'll be shattered for the rest of the week. At larger parties, latecomers are at their most menacing. They think it isn't cool to be on time. There'll be nobody there anywhere. So there is always that grinding, underpopulated first hour, awful for the hosts. The late-comers' idea is that they are leaving it to others to get the party going.

So next time you say to a latecomer, 'Oh, don't worry. It's quite all right,' remember you've just let someone smash up a social occasion.

Or it could be worse. Finally, Matt confesses all. He and Lucy have given up having people round in the week *altogether* because guests were never on time and the whole thing went on too late. There we have it. Latecomers don't just muck up present enjoyment. They destroy future fun as well.

Here are some remedies:

- With friends who are late meeting up out somewhere, be ruthless. If they are more than fifteen minutes late for the third time in a row, don't wait another minute. Go home. Go off and amuse yourself elsewhere. With some people lateness is a symptom of general unreliability and selfishness. You might have to get rid of them altogether. But it isn't always. Sometimes they reform. Always give them a chance if they promise to do better.

- If people are coming round to your house, you could follow the example of a lady called Mrs Robson Scott. She simply refused admission. 'You're too late,' she would inform them on the doorstep. This is extreme.
- Start without them. Why not? Don't offer to recap any missed courses, either. It might be awkward the once, but they'll learn their lesson. People hate missing out.
- Be decisive at the inviting stage. Make the time most distinctly a part of the invitation. 'Would you mind coming at 7.30, because so-and-so has to go off early next morning on a business trip?' Or you can make a joke of it. 'There'll be nothing left if you don't come on time.' Target known latecomers.
- Include disparaging remarks about latecomers into your general conversation.
- Don't expect immediate results. Gradually, not being late will become popular, especially when people see that it makes social life possible.

I could have danced all night!

I'm sure you could.

It's not just the fault of latecomers that social occasions these days sprawl so ruthlessly over vast tracts of time. We all conspire to keep the hour late or long. No decent party is ever supposed to end. 'Until late' it says on the invitation and when is 'late'?

We live like the leisured aristocracy of nineteenth-century imperial Russia, who didn't have to get up in the morning.

Weddings last for days, weekend lunch is over at midnight, a night out, especially if clubbing is involved, careers significantly into the following day.

And why not? People are having a good time. What's the problem? Zoe doesn't see one. If she's got to go to work the next day, she has her means of survival. Not even Matt wants to be a party pooper or a boring person who has to be tucked up in bed by midnight.

This is why he is often to be seen at parties, slumped in a chair, past it. But he admits to nothing.

Unlikely as it may seem, it is Zoe who makes the damaging admission: 'There's a lot of pressure. It's like people are saying you're only having a good time if you stay out really really late. Sometimes I get fed up with it.'

That is interesting.

How often does it happen that one guest making a move to leave inspires a great cluck of departure in all the others who, it turns out, have been waiting for the opportunity?

They have become a tyranny, these late and long hours. We feel obliged to stay – if we don't, the hosts will be upset, the party won't really have been a success. How many people, who would love to have a busy day brightened by two hours of socialising, don't dare go out because they know it'll be four? And perhaps the feeling is mutual. Perhaps people don't ask their friends round for the same reason?

There is a person who has his lights rigged up on a timer so that they switch off in a dismissive fashion at 10.30. If this fails to turf them out, he will appear with a vacuum cleaner. We don't have to go that far but:

- If the invitation says 6.00 to 10.00 or 6.00 to 8.00 maybe that is what it means.
- Leave *before* your useful life as a guest has come to an end.
- Don't be guilty about leaving. It's not unreasonable to go home at 10.30 on a weekday, maybe 11.00 on a Saturday. Don't let hosts make you feel bad.

What's wrong with social life that refreshes rather than debilitates? Brevity could lead to rigor. It could be like speed dating. Instead of sprawling about getting drunk, people will make more effort if they know that time is limited.

Late hosts

Sometimes it is the hosts who are late.

'A good hostess never allows the wheels of her domestic machinery to be seen,' an old etiquette book decrees. Modern informality is such that the wheels may well be all you'll see.

Matt once went to dinner and was dragooned into making the beds. On another red-face-making occasion (How many can a man have?) he and Lucy had to leave before the pudding because of the babysitter. 'I knew what was coming when we arrived and they said they were only just back from the supermarket.'

It's harsh, it's cruel, but it's got to be said – and it's good for you – hosts, you don't have to be perfect, but you can't, you just can't be drastically late with the food. You may not mean it, but it isn't hospitable, it isn't friendly.

- On weekdays, you need to have your dinner on the table by 8.30 at the absolute latest if guests are going to be able to leave by 10.30 or 11.00 and on Saturdays it should be 9.00. If you fail in everything else, don't fail in this.
- Sometimes guests are asked to *arrive* at 8.30 for a weekday dinner. This may suit you but it'll be too late for your guests. Prepare the day before if you're going to be back late from work.
- People with young children must not be kept up late. Remember, they will be bashed awake at 6.00, come what may.

For advice on how to save time and avoid delay, see **What shall I give them? Food for others**, page 116.

Food and Menu Manners

What shall I give them? Food for others

Nothing is more anxiety inducing. 'If I had ten minutes to prepare a major presentation at work, I think I'd cope better than if someone said, "Eight people are coming through the door for dinner",' Matt confesses. Even Zoe, who would never bother with anything you might call a dinner party, is subject to stage fright in the kitchen. Once she nearly threw some Bolognese sauce out of the window: 'It was taking such bloody ages to cook.'

Only Mrs Gibbs is more serene. 'At my age I don't really bother but I remember when my husband was alive I'd be at my wits' end. But then we were trying to pretend we'd still got servants. I had to do all the cooking in full evening dress. It's all quite different now, isn't it, with these kitchen suppers?'

If only this were true. In recent years, 'entertaining' has once again become, in the eyes of some hosts, a status-promoting opportunity to intimidate the guests. So some of us have got this self-imposed challenge to meet. On top of this, we have had the 'food revolution' – the River Café, Nigella, Jamie. Cooking is enough of a worry as it is – few jobs have deadlines as immovable or requiring so many aspects to be perfectly coordinated. Things have never been worse.

And of course, modern, relaxed hosts want it all to look effortless. Nothing is more guaranteed to stiffen your guests than the sense, leaking like gas under the door, of a crisis in the kitchen.

How to avoid all this torment and misery:

- KNOW YOUR OWN STRENGTH.
- Don't forget, your guests have come for the company. Good cooking may be appreciated as a feature of dinners in some homes, but other dinners may have other features.
- Non-cooks can and must have people round. Robert Tibbles, the collector of Young British Art, is a perfect example. He can just about manage some kind of pasta in tomato sauce. Otherwise it's Marks & Spencer through and through. When some very grand people came to visit his art collection they were given takeaway pizza. He offers this food without apology and expects no comment, favourable or otherwise.
- Some non-cooks cower away from returning the hospitality of people they consider cooks. DON'T. M & S or Tesco's Finest are perfectly delightful.
- Some non-cooks, or people too grand or important to

visit shops, employ 'dinner party services' or caterers at vast expense. The food is often only a notch or two better than ready meals from the supermarket (might even *be* ready meals from the supermarket, in fact) and some guests find the presence of 'staff' intimidating. Besides, it's a homely touch if you've heated it up yourself.

- Trouble only sets in when non-cooks forget that they are non-cooks.

Cooks will look for greater challenges. But, please, not too great. Your guests want to see more of you than of your apron strings endlessly retreating into the kitchen. Don't end up like the poor woman Nigella Lawson went to dinner with, whose menu was so unmanageably elaborate that, during the gargantuan pauses between the courses, she was to be heard sobbing in the kitchen.

So, for your own sake:

- Stick to recipes that you have done before.
- Choose dishes whose ingredients are in season or are easily available. Don't be wretchedly middle class like Matt and have to drive all over Lincolnshire looking for kaffir lime leaves. 'I didn't even know what they were,' he said.
- Make sure you have the utensils to cook the planned dishes.
- Choose food that can mostly be prepared in advance and is easy to serve.

- No potatoes – this is Nigella Lawson's idea. No boring scrubbing or peeling.
- Why do there have to be three courses? Who says?

For the sake of your guests:

- No small bones.
- No sloppy food – guests splattering themselves.
- No offal – often not liked.
- Be careful about seafood and hot spicy food.
- No food that might look off-putting – remember Matt's unfortunate experience with that mackerel cooked in tea. 'I won't tell you what it looked like,' he says.

Eat it up!

Mrs Gibbs is of the generation that grinned and bore it. 'At school we had to eat what we were given and that was that. I only drew the line on Friday which was a horrifying grey slab of rice pudding – and, of course, the skin – but luckily it was so solid you could pick it up and get it into your pocket. But as a grown-up I've been grateful for the training. If someone gives me something I don't like the look of, I just buckle to and get it down. It's saved many an embarrassing situation. The food in Britain was pretty filthy during the war and for years afterwards, I can tell you.'

She would go along with Nancy Mitford. At a palatially grand dinner in Venice in the 1950s the author was sitting next to a nervous young man. He took a mouthful of lobster, went white and turned to her (ignoring, in the crisis, the rule about not talking with your mouth full): 'What shall I do? I think it's off. Shall I spit it out?' Her reply: 'Swallow it, if it kills you.'

Alas, no more! Now we have the pickers-out. 'Olives and sultanas,' Matt says. 'You can guarantee some wimp will pick them out. Why do they always line them up in a neat row round the edge of the plate?' Zoe, although she doesn't know it, annoys her friends with her food fads – she doesn't like avocados, mozzarella cheese, white chocolate or anchovies. But apparently if you cook anchovy into something, she doesn't notice.

- Fussy eaters have never been popular. They're life denying. They can't be taken seriously. Don't be one of them.
- There's no call, these days, to leave 'something for Mr Manners'. Astonishingly, a very young person told me of someone he knows who thinks it polite to leave a piece of everything on his plate – a morsel of meat, half a potato and nine peas. He will even accept 'seconds' in order to do this. Bring on the men in white coats!

Special orders

Matt is worried. 'Whose job is it to ask about special diets and so on – the host or the guest?'

Answer: the guest.

- When accepting the invitation, the guest should explain if there are certain foods they absolutely can't eat. If hosts ask, absurd or embarrassing situations can occur: 'I'm not awfully fond of squirrel,' or 'I can't touch caviar,' implying that the guest expects food of that luxury to be offered. To some guests, the enquiry is an invitation to list a great baroque panoply of food fads. The question can induce anxiety. You think, 'Maybe there's something I just can't stand, but I can't quite remember what it is.'

- You don't actually have to produce a doctor's certificate, but special dietary requirements should be of a medical, ideological or religious nature. If you're dieting to lose weight, you can either refuse the invitation or accept and eat only a little of whatever is on offer. Hosts cannot be expected to mug up on the Atkins Diet or the Carol Vorderman detox diet just for you.

- Don't bang on about your diet once you're actually there, either, unless you want to trample on everybody else's pleasure in eating and the hosts' pleasure in providing food.

- If you are vegetarian, it's very helpful if you explain what kind – fish eating or not, or even if you merely mean that you don't eat red meat. Hosts might feel awkward about asking, fearing a rocket from true practitioners.

- Hosts, don't assume it's plain-sailing once you've got the special orders. Zoe once hospitalised someone with nut allergy. 'It was the groundnut oil. I just didn't think that would be nuts.' Nancy Mitford's dictum, 'Swallow it if it kills you,' shouldn't be taken literally.

- It's easy to be caught out with vegetarians, too. Just because it isn't meat doesn't mean it hasn't got an animal product in it somewhere – certain cheeses, for example.
- Sometimes it is thought that bacon, just because it is lurking in the background of a dish, won't be noticed or objected to by Muslims, Jews or vegetarians. Matt, arriving early once, found the hostess trying to obliterate this item from a peculiar-sounding fruit sauce she was making for a Jewish guest. She was whizzing it up in the liquidiser. She was persuaded to start again.
- People on special diets can either be given separate food or the whole menu can be planned around their requirements. Whatever you do, give them something decent to eat. The practice of palming vegetarians off with 'just the vegetables' while everybody else tucks into a splendid roast dinner is now frowned upon.
- But you could do this if you were actually anti-vegetarian.

Sitting-down-to-eat Manners

What's on the table

Needless to say, Matt gets in a flap about the cutlery. 'I *do* know you're supposed to start on the outside and work in. It's incredibly embarrassing when you have to be given another fork because you've already used it.'

Extraordinary, the things people worry about.

- If you're interested – you're *supposed* to start with the cutlery on the outside and work in. But why not make a point of getting it wrong?
- It is so much more plain and square and English if the pudding spoon and fork are laid across *the top* of the place setting rather than everything at the side, which is somehow characterless, international and restaurant.
- Why not keep cutlery in short supply so that your visitors have to use the same knife and fork throughout? This is the way at Zoe's place where guests always feel at home.
- Something to wipe your mouth with is not daintiness

but essential. Only the house mates in *Big Brother* are content to do without. If you have to have cloth napkins, the unironed and threadbare (but clean) variety is best. Otherwise, kitchen paper is perfect.

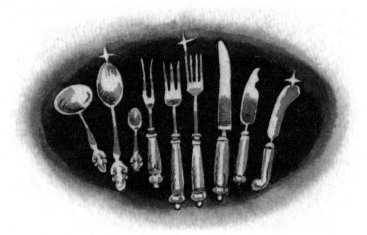

- If you have anything that might be called a table decoration, throw it away. Apart from candles. 'We were given some weird china flowers in baskets for a wedding present,' says Matt. 'But somebody knocked them on the floor.' What a mercy!
- Put the wine and water in bottles on the table and leave the guests to get on with it.

'Placement'

Whatever you do, don't call it that. At Zoe's there is never a seating plan. Matt has one but it gets lost or is misremembered. But people like a seating plan. It relieves them of responsibility. Also, you don't have couples sitting next to each other, the sexes in separate clumps, the shy guests marginalised.

- If you're really clever, you can memorise a thoughtful arrangement and get guests into their places without fuss, glossing over what might otherwise seem stage-managed. It is better to say, 'Would you like to sit . . . ?' rather than 'You're sitting . . .' Name places or a diagram openly consulted by the hosts if there are just six or eight make too much of a meal of it.
- At very large sit-down dos, the seating plan needs to be displayed in visual form near the door. Otherwise guests are scrabbling around looking for their places.

'Wiring in'

'We're always telling people to start as soon as they're served,' says Matt, 'but they never do.' Strangely, it would be a different story if he had Mrs Gibbs to dinner. 'In the days before central heating, food was always stone-cold by the time you'd waited politely for everybody to be served. I've a horror of it. I always wire in straight away, whether invited to or not.'

- Why not get the beauty of it hot? If you're invited to begin (ignore that last remark of Mrs Gibbs's), begin.

Slow eaters

- When slow eaters say, 'Don't wait for me,' they should be obeyed. Hosts can then get on with doling out 'seconds'.

Table manners

Table manners were the worst of old manners. Excessive daintiness with the napkin, tipping the soup plate away from the person, spooning the soup away from the person, constantly offering to pass dishes, water, salt to your neighbour – if anyone did all this now, we'd think they were mental. But still the shadow persists. Even quite young people react with a gasp of guilt when asked to pass something – as if they should have noticed what was needed in the first place. People are worried about their table manners.

- No need to feel guilty if asked to pass something. You don't have to sit there in a heightened state of alert, thinking only of others.
- No need to feel awkward about asking for something to be passed.
- Pick up bones in your fingers – but avoid dog-like gnawing.
- It is quite all right to mop up sauce or oil from your plate

with a piece of bread, a practice once thought revoltingly foreign, but now a compliment to the cook.

· You can put your elbows on the table.

Nasty eating habits

'I'm quite happy to say goodbye to all that nonsense about how to hold your knife and fork,' Mrs Gibbs says, 'but I don't care for people talking with their mouths full, which is what my great-nieces do, of course, and a lord I once came across – who you would have thought would know better.' Her great-nieces also 'have the most extraordinary way of eating generally. Their faces are practically in the plate, the fork is lined up right in front of their mouths so that the food can be loaded straight in – all very convenient, no doubt, but really I'd rather watch a dog eat.' This, of course, is how Zoe eats. It's a consequence of living in flat shares where you pick from the fridge, or eat standing up or sitting in front of the TV.

· It isn't agreeable sitting next to someone who talks with their mouth full or who has unpleasant eating habits.
· Unfortunately, only an intimate can point this out – and should do so. That is what intimates are for.

Food stuck on the face

'It's incredibly embarrassing when someone gets a bit of food stuck on their face,' says Matt. Yes, isn't it. Here's what you do:

- Use your own napkin or piece of kitchen paper to scrub quietly but persistently at the same part of your own face. Shortly, you will find your co-diner doing the same to their own face – quite unconsciously. It always works like magic.

Do we mention the food?

In old manners the rule was that no mention should be made of the food, let alone compliments offered. But there was a reason for this. Mrs Bridges or her equivalent produced very dull food and it was always the same. Dinner in one house was more or less identical to dinner in another. There was no point in mentioning it.

Today it is different but people still don't know what to do. Matt worries. 'Will it just sound polite? Just going through the motions? And what if it's really horrible?' He is, of course, thinking of that mackerel in cold tea again.

- Always mention the food but don't worry – you don't have to be insincere. Producers of inedible food aren't that bothered anyway and won't notice that appreciation is no more than polite.

- Where genuine enthusiasm can be expressed, it should be. Good cooks will accept lukewarm praise as fair comment.
- Cooks – don't apologise for a mistake unless you are prepared for the guests to agree.
- Perhaps as a result of the mackerel trauma, Matt developed a habit of offering fulsome praise *before* he had taken a mouthful – until a sharp-eyed hostess caught him out one day. Don't follow this example.
- Where the dinner is bought in (or BI to use the correct expression), the hosts should declare this and not expect compliments, although to offer them would not be wrong. Don't, under any circumstances, attempt to pass off BI as your own; you're bound to be exposed sooner or later, as Linda Snell was in *The Archers*, when Eddie Grundy got into her kitchen and found the boxes.

Wine talk

Unless all the guests are wine snobs, or the dinner has been especially convened for the purpose (in which case most of us wouldn't be there), wine talk should be kept to a minimum. Nothing more ghastly than one dinner where one of the guests insisted not just on bringing all the wine herself but also on grilling the other diners imperiously about it. Anybody unable to identify a particular wine was condemned as not fit to drink it.

Drunkenness

Guests, and hosts for that matter, should not get drunk but intermittently they do. You can try withdrawing the supply, but some guests are not above shrilly demanding more once they've got going. Then what do you do?

- Either strategically ignore requests for more.
- Or become expert at using the operation of pretending to refill the glass as a cover for actually whisking it away.

Breakages must be paid for

Usually, it's as bad as it possibly could be. A friend of mine, taken to meet his girlfriend's family for the first time, thought he would be helpful. Carrying the sauce-boat into the kitchen, he somehow managed to slip. The sauce-boat flew backwards, into the dining room. The grandmother only got her new glasses whipped off and smashed to the ground. But the rather frightening mother of the girlfriend was less fortunate. In addition to being well coated in sauce, she sustained a black eye. And, on landing, the missile, of course, crashed into and destroyed the vegetable dish which was part of the best dinner service which had been in the family for generations, had been given to the great-grandparents as a wedding present etc. . . . .

Almost a thousand pounds' worth of damage was done, not including any claims for injury or psychological trauma. What was my friend to do? Sit down and write a cheque there and then? One approach, unfortunately not possible on this occasion, was demonstrated by Dixon in *Lucky Jim*. He burnt a huge hole in a blanket while staying overnight at his boss's house; so he stuffed it into the airing cupboard and hoped for the best. But only a few days later the boss's wife was booming down the telephone, demanding an explanation.

- Always offer to pay if you break or damage something. The offer should always be refused.
- If guests break things, it is never their fault – often it really isn't. There's a loose floorboard you ought to have fixed months ago or the table wobbles or you've put something in a silly place where it's bound to get knocked over.
- Hosts should live with the risk of china and glass (especially) getting broken. If it's unspeakably priceless and it would kill you if it got broken, *don't use it*.

Returning-hospitality Manners: also the Problem of Richer Friends

Do we dare to ask them back?

Major-liberation, D-Day-style operations are called for here.

Scroungers and meanies are one thing. There was a couple in Notting Hill who took to showing up at a friend's home at mealtimes at least three times a week. After many months of this, and that friend never having been asked back, they suddenly made a remarkable offer. 'Hey, look, if you go to the supermarket and buy a chicken, *we'll cook it for you.*'

This kind of thing is rare.

More frequent is this. Matt is speaking: 'I get on really well with one of my colleagues but the trouble is he's independently wealthy and entertains a lot. Last year we went to him three times but he only came to us once. I feel really bad about that.'

Or this. New friends are invited round a couple of times.

Everything appears to go well. And then . . . nothing. You're never asked back. They're never heard of again. Matt, tragically, in these circumstances, assumes that the people don't like him. But the real reason is probably sadder and even more sinister. Those would-be friends, burdened with the horrible British idea that hospitality must be repaid in kind and feeling, for whatever reason, unequal to the task, just run away and hide.

This is awful.

The 'thinking' goes: if you're a non-cook, you can't return the hospitality of cooks; if you're less well off, perhaps younger, you daren't invite older, better-off people. It only looks like lack of confidence; really it's mean and competitive: 'They did fillet steak and parma ham; we'd better lob back with something better than Spag Bol.'

- Let's get rid of this ghastly tit-for-tat approach to hospitality. The idea of people dutifully lobbing invitations back and forth at each other in strict rotation is deadly. If you phone up and invite someone and they start twittering, 'Oh, but it's really our turn,' just say, 'We're not counting.'
- Even more radical – this ghastly idea that hospitality can only be repaid *in kind*, has got to go.
- Non-cooks should not hesitate to invite cooks (see **What shall I give them? Food for others**, page 116).
- The rich should be grateful for the hospitality of the less well off.
- Why not escape the whole sad middle-class dinner-party

treadmill altogether? Repay hospitality with a trip to the dogs, an ice-rink, a bowling alley. Anything – it really doesn't matter.

What if your friends are hugely richer than you?

Don't let anything stand in your way.

The kind of mega-billionaires who live in one room with sticky tape over the broken window-panes and eat fish and chips out of the wrapping paper present no social difficulties. Usually, they are chronically reclusive, so you won't even know them. But what about the rich for whom being rich is a way of life? The ones who, when an airline makes a fuss about their trying to book four seats for their children in first class (they might disturb the other passengers), find a simple solution: book the whole of first class. Or whose conversation is about how it costs them £4,000 an hour to fly their jet, of which they have two, one for internal use and one for intercontinental – ocean-going, as it were – oh, and they're planning a third, especially adapted for landing on golf courses.

What do you do if people like this are your friends? And you're someone like Matt, not badly off, just a touch competitive, remortgaging fairly often to raise extra cash but, there's no getting away from it, *just not in the same league.*

Well, most rich people have the gumption to realise that if they're going to have any friends at all they'll have to pay for everything. His rich friend at work, Matthew, invites

Matt and Lucy every year to some glamorous holiday villa in Tuscany or Greece. All they have to fork out for is easyJet. In between, they get gorgeous outings to the Ivy, the River Café, the Savoy Grill, and Matt gets fabulous tickets for Arsenal matches.

And all the time, he's doing Matthew a favour. Without him, he and his wife would be terribly lonely.

If your friends are vastly richer than you, you should think yourself bloody lucky! Rejoice! Don't let anything stand in your way. But just one word of warning. Only take up the following suggestions if your friends are really and truly excessively rich.

- Don't let uncalled-for guilt spoil it all. Don't be damp and depressing like Matt. Remember – they can afford it. The only thing is, in restaurants, you should have what you want, regardless of cost – *but* it might be a bit shameless to order Beluga caviar or a whole lobster.

- You can certainly invite your rich friends to your home but don't try to compete with them. In fact, it is a good idea to make economy a theme. Offer very cheap dishes – Lancashire hot-pot or something made of mince – and keep the conversation sternly anchored to such subjects as sale bargains, budget airlines and energy-saving light bulbs; you might have a pile of holey socks to hand which you can conspicuously darn throughout. Rich people rather enjoy all this; it makes a nice change for them.
- Rich people always have a pathetic side. They don't know how to get on a tube train or a bus. They can barely dress themselves and know nothing of dusting or hoovering. They should always be treated in a bantering, slightly patronising way as if they were delicate children, especially when they come to your house: 'I do hope you can manage the stairs; we can't really stretch to a lift just yet. In fact, stairs are a bit of an extravagance, to be honest.'
- But they do also have to be indulged, just a little. It's quite likely that they will arrive at your home with several hundred pounds' worth of wine in a special basket. You have to make an exception to the rule about not feeling obliged to open such gifts then and there (see **Do I bring a bottle?**, page 224). Their offering will be at least partly for their own benefit, which is fair enough. They really can't be expected to manage on cheap drink. Anything costing less than £15 a bottle upsets their stomachs.
- You should perhaps give your rich friends rather more

gifts than you might your other friends, but don't make any special effort as to quality. Ms Lillian Carter, the mother of the former President, had the right idea when she presented to Estée Lauder a gift of grits (roughly the American equivalent of porridge). 'I just thought of the one thing you wouldn't have,' she said.

- If you can manage it (but you must on no account bust the bank for your rich friends – what is the point?), it is a good idea to very occasionally come up with some quite astonishing gift – something almost on their level – perhaps £400 worth of opera tickets or an entire dinner service (which you got in a sale, of course). A little indulgence on your credit card might allow these things. But don't do it too often, otherwise you will be bankrupt and your rich friends will only see it as competition.

- But small gifts and the occasional big one give much pleasure to rich people because normally nobody gives them anything.

Names Manners

Names, names, names

When Zoe was a schoolgirl, her head teacher thought it would be good preparation for something or other if she were to meet Lord Justice Elizabeth Butler-Sloss, who was to present prizes, at the station. But she could have been better briefed. She approached who she hoped was the right small, friendly-looking woman and said rather too loudly, 'Excuse me, are you Lord Justice Butler-Sloss?' Even in the busy suburban station in the rush hour, heads turned at the oddity of it. How was she to know that the correct way of addressing this particular *lady* lord is 'Dame Elizabeth' – who was most forbearing about the mistake.

At one time, mistakes of this kind were fatal – a sure sign that you didn't belong. Nowadays, it isn't just that we couldn't care less, we actually relish opportunities to get it wrong. But they never come. Where are all the titled people? When again in her life is Zoe going to be fetching a Lord Justice or the equivalent from the station?

Our trouble with names is remembering them at all. As we already know, Matt has a terrible time, often not remembering the person, let alone the name. 'But they *always* remember me. Why?' he complains. Perhaps he should be flattered (see **Chance encounters**, page 26).

Social life, in tune with the economy, has grown and grown in recent years. We meet more people – more names to forget. On top of that, a new idea that a poor head for names is a 'symptom', perhaps of a drastic inability to form meaningful relationships (Zoe, like many young people, damn them, never forgets a name – a useful knack in the PR world) is fighting it out with the traditional British feeling that calling someone you don't know very well by their name is just too intimate and intrusive – almost as bad as striking up a conversation with a stranger on the bus. And if you don't call someone by their name when you first meet, the chances are you'll forget it.

What are we to do?

- There is the American method of repeating names when first introduced. This is supposed to aid the memory as well as being fantastically friendly. Matt has tried it. 'I thought people were looking at me oddly. I'm not sure . . .' Exactly, we're not American. If you start that up, people will think there's something wrong with you. It's too forward, too brash – and too obvious. You could try being a little more subtle about it, starting to use the person's name quietly, a little later in the conversation – but by then you will have forgotten it anyway.

- Never say, 'I'm sorry, I don't remember your name.' Nobody likes not being remembered. It always feels like a more fundamental cancellation (see **Chance encounters**, page 26).

- Sometimes, there's a chance to get away and return later, suddenly knowing the name – you've asked somebody else.

- Resort to subterfuge. Be prepared. Work out who is likely to be at a particular party who you've met before but only remember as 'the olive-oil salesman' or 'keen on bats' or 'went on holiday to Croatia'. Plot to find out their names in advance. This is an amusing game in itself.

- If caught by surprise (and we usually are), try to corner the host or another likely guest for an unobtrusive briefing.

- If you have forgotten someone's name, it is a certainty that they will have remembered yours. This must be a law of social life yet to be properly understood and named.

- A nightmare situation is where your mind goes blank just as you are about to introduce someone whose name you know perfectly well. Mercifully, more and more people are coming to the rescue by stepping in and giving their names themselves, before the full horror of the situation is revealed. This is most tactful. So, make sure you have your name ready (and haven't forgotten it) when being introduced, because sudden, devastating memory loss often strikes introducers.

- Try Mrs Gibbs's method. She is blessed with poor eyesight

in old age. Without her glasses she can't see a thing. 'I say, "I've left my glasses behind. You'll have to tell me who you are." Once I realised too late that I'd actually got my glasses on.'

That's not my name!

'My name is Matt,' says Matt. 'Nobody calls me Matthew, except my wife when there's a row on. But my rich friend at work is actually Matthew. He hates being called Matt but people are always doing it.' This isn't being stuck-up. After all, we haven't yet heard of 'Dave' Beckham and his wife, Vikki.

- Don't abbreviate a name unless it is clear the person prefers this. It may be trendy to lop bits off names with hideous results, especially amongst the under thirties, but not every Catherine has to be a Cat or every Anthony an Ant. Zoe, of course, is called 'Zo' or 'Zzzz'. How long before every name has been reduced to a single letter, to be sounded like a foreigner learning the English alphabet? 'This is Mr "T" Blair.' 'You have met Queen "E".' Primitive but energy saving.

More than one name: Nicknames and the in-crowd question

Matt is troubled by a couple he knows. They have three names: Katherine and Charles or Kate and Chaz and also (to certain of their friends but not their offspring) 'Mum and Dad'. 'I don't know them as Mum and Dad but some of their other friends call them that when they're talking to me. It makes me feel a bit out of it . . .'

Of course it does.

- Avoid 'in' nicknames when talking to people who aren't in.
- Vent your fury if someone refers to a well-known person either by a nickname or even by their first name alone. This is ghastly name-dropping (see **Name-dropping**, page 160). Someone should tell politicians that referring to 'Tony' or 'Gordon' in interviews doesn't create a nice cosy friendly feel. Quite the opposite. It sounds like snotty name-dropping and listeners and viewers feel excluded.
- Strike back with a dose of their own medicine. Dead famous people (actually dead, not 'dead famous') are ideal – much harder for others to check up on. You can say, 'Poor Grace, I've never got over it, you know.'

Call me what you like – I don't mind

In Matt's office there are quite a few people whose names are never pronounced right – mainly by him. There is a 'Maya' which should be pronounced 'My-ya' and a 'Rakhee' which has a short rather than long 'a'. Asian names, you see. Both these women have given up. 'My-ya' or 'Maya', 'Rakhee' or 'Raakhee'; 'I don't mind,' they say, but not exactly to his face. But Matt is a sensitive soul. If he knew what was happening, it might just be that he would feel a little bit of a white colonialist tramping all over someone's name.

Amongst the under thirties there is a similar relativism about names. People allow their names to be mangled, lopped and contorted in whatever way the passer-by fancies. I heard of a new colleague with an unusual name. When asked which of two plausible but very different pronunciations was the right one she actually said, 'I don't mind.' Now everybody thinks this poor girl is a terrible drip with no opinions about anything!

- If it's a matter of 'Kan*i*ka' (emphasis on the second syllable) or '*Kan*ika' (emphasis on the first) or 'Thulasy' (the *h* not pronounced), be gently insistent that your name is pronounced correctly.
- But insisting on the exact nuances of pronunciation could be cruel as well as pointless. If you have a completely impossible name (some Polish surnames, for instance, or the Vietnamese surname 'Ng'), you might have to accept that people are doing their best.

- Resist the trend, not exclusive to ethnic minorities and rampant amongst Zoe's friends and people under thirty, of having no particular name. Zoe's friend Natasha is so flexi-named: 'Nat' or 'Tasha' or even 'Tash'. Decide who you are and stick to it.

What-to-say Manners

Getting to know people: Perfect questions

(The late) Lord Rothermere said to the artist, Francis Bacon, who was often an awkward customer, 'What do you do?' He replied, 'I'm an old queen.'

'What do you do?' 'What do you do?' We hear this particular axe being wielded all the time nowadays. Even Mrs Gibbs has been subject to it. It is Zoe's favourite conversational opener; she's never given it much thought, to tell the truth, but it sounds sociable enough to her. Matt, on the other hand, is usually on the receiving end and he doesn't like it. 'Sometimes you get a real grilling. "What do you do?" "Where do you live?" "Where do the children go to school?" It's really embarrassing, especially when everybody stops to listen to your answers.' Someone even asked, on first meeting, 'What do you weigh?'

Matt is absolutely right. 'What do you do?' isn't a friendly question at all. People should be more honest and ask what they really want to know: 'What class are you?' 'How much money have you got?' 'Do you amount to anything or are you a nobody?'

Has 'What do you do?' ever led to interesting conversation?

- People feel trapped by questions demanding information, demanding more than yes or no.
- But gentle questions that *only* require yes or no will produce more expansive responses. If you say, 'Do you have a difficult journey to work?' the person is likely to be 'prompted' to say more, perhaps even to reveal what they do.
- 'Do you *happen to* have a dog?' 'Are you *by any chance* interested in field mice?' These phrases remove any hard expectation that the person ought or ought not to have a dog or be interested in field mice.
- Too many people today apply 'skills' learned from assertiveness-training courses at work to their social life.

'Where are you from?' We've got into an amazing muddle about this. Matt and Zoe would freeze in horror at the very idea of it, although they have been asked the question themselves. The question is taboo, must never be asked of members of ethnic minorities or indeed anybody at all. It's too sensitive, there are too many issues of race and class to be trodden on. Yet, the other day, Mrs Gibbs, who shares none of these anxieties, discovered someone who, like her, had lived in Bournemouth as a child and shared her passion for the place. It was extraordinary they had never met before. They had a whale of a time recalling the old days.

But most of us have become people without a background, people from nowhere.

Even if somebody boldly indicates that they are quite willing to talk about where they are from, if they say, 'When my family came from Uganda in the 1970s . . .' or 'My grandparents were born in Malaysia . . .' those around are likely to turn rigid with embarrassment. 'It seems all wrong to me,' says Matt. 'It's best to avoid the whole subject.'

- 'Where are you from?' is offensive if the implication is clearly (and how clear it often is), 'You can't be British.'
- Or if it appears to be a reaction to someone's appearance or way of speaking. If Zoe starts talking posh, which she does sometimes for reasons best known to herself, somebody might ask her where she is from. She replies truthfully, 'Ashton under Lyne.' The same thing happens to Matt when the only remaining traces of his northern accent (he comes from Hartlepool) are heard, when he says 'bus' or 'us'.
- That aside, let's have more talking about where we're from. We should initiate it ourselves. It's pointless waiting to be asked. What holds us back – is it snobbery? Be generous, give of yourself and others will do the same.

The other phenomenon of modern life is no questions at all. 'It usually only hits you when you get home,' says Matt. 'You've met someone new and they told funny stories and talked about TV but you don't realise that they didn't ask you a single question about yourself until afterwards. You end up thinking, "What's the point? I might as well never have met that person." It's quite depressing.'

Ah, so, by the sound of it, you didn't ask any questions either . . .

The alienation of the modern world, our innate selfishness – there are all kinds of glamorous explanations for this failure to connect. But most likely it is down to plain old confusion and uncertainty. We can't see any alternative to the 'What do you do?' routine, which we know is naff and grim.

And we don't know how else to go about it. We don't know how to ask questions.

So the simplest solution is to batten down. Avoid the whole issue. Ask no questions at all.

Young people have always had a terrifying intolerance of the whole business of 'getting to know you', anyway. Somebody once asked Zoe, 'Do you live near here?' and she replied, 'Can't you think of anything more original than that?'

- Don't be embarrassed to ask 'boring' questions. You've got to start somewhere. People (except Zoe) appreciate *any* interest being taken in them – or ought to.
- Ask indirect questions. Avoid grilling. (See above for ways of doing this.)
- It is more boring, in the long run, to find out nothing about someone.

'What have you been up to recently?' is at least a question, but it's a dud. Matt's mind goes blank. 'Once I was so desperate, I said, "I'm just back from the car wash."' Zoe, while not disconcerted, jabbers mindlessly: 'I'm really great. Having a great time . . .' and so on.

* Don't ask, 'What have you been up to recently?'

Interrupting

Zoe is always interrupting, Mrs Gibbs is always being interrupted. Zoe interrupts if she is bored. She doesn't usually know she is doing it. But if someone is talking about their holiday she does. 'I may be old but I don't repeat myself. I've made sure of that,' says Mrs Gibbs. 'But I only have to utter about two and a half sentences and someone will be sure to interrupt. I blame TV.' Matt doesn't interrupt, but he notices others doing it, 'usually just when the conversation is getting interesting'.

Interrupting can take the form of cutting someone off before they have finished speaking or changing the subject prematurely. Mrs Gibbs talks interestingly about the issues of the day; she listens to Radio 4; she is alarmingly well informed. Perhaps this is why she has to be interrupted. She is too much of a threat. An argument could break out (see **Let's have a heated debate**, page 153). Others interrupt because they prefer to be talking themselves, or because they're not paying attention, or both.

In one way and another, interrupting is quite a serious

social disease. 'Sometimes at the end of the evening, you feel that nothing really happened, the conversation never really got going, it was all over the place,' says Matt. Yes, an expressionist nightmare – a row of birds sitting on a telephone wire all twittering away to themselves.

- Don't interrupt.
- Be patient. If you're bored, endure until it's the right moment to subtly wheel the conversation round to another subject.

See also **Surviving the stand-up party**, page 173.

Am I boring?

Matt and Mrs Gibbs are not boring. To be honest, Zoe sometimes is.

The most boring people:

- Are brilliantly amusing.
- When not being brilliantly amusing, talk brilliantly.
- Tell the most marvellous anecdotes.
- Make an awesome display of their knowledge.

Why is it that we want to clobber them? Because we haven't got a word in edgeways, we've been made to feel ignorant, we've found out nothing, we've been intimidated, we've been ignored. In a word, we're crushed.

- To be truly boring, make sure you take no interest whatsoever in other people.

Putting your foot in it

We've all done it and it's murder and you never forget it. The worst of a gaffe is that you didn't mean it, it was an awful accident, you're not really like that. But remember, being contorted with embarrassment and shame is what saves you.

Matt had a terrible experience: 'We were round at some people we didn't know very well and it was a bit heavy going at the start. I don't know what happened but I suddenly found myself going on and on about spinach which I really hate. And guess what was for dinner. That's right. Spinach tart!'

Zoe, on the other hand, said to a woman she works with, 'You must tell me all about the Second World War.'

'But I wasn't born,' the woman screamed and clutched at her face, as if administering an instant lift.

The awful thing is, Zoe didn't even notice.

Sometimes the victim will spit back. Estée Lauder was enraged when a well-known decorator said she 'could do wonders' with the vast baronial hallway of the Lauder residence in Manhattan. Estée seized the poor woman's 'sagging cheeks' and said, 'I could do wonders with these.'

- Generous hearers can disperse the gaseous cloud from some gaffes. When Matt railed against spinach, a bold host might have taken the bull by the horns and said, 'Well, you'll find our spinach tart pure torture, won't you?' And then they could all have had fun watching him try to eat it. It might have made the evening.

- Or the one responsible for the gaffe can say, 'That came out all wrong. I didn't mean to say . . . I don't at all mean . . .' and firmly correct the impression given.
- But others are hopeless cases and, like stains, only get worse from rubbing. At times there is nothing to be done. Don't try to cover up the gaffe and don't try to cover up your embarrassment either or people might think you're the kind of insensitive yob who says these awful things and *doesn't even realise*.

Ideally, we should avoid gaffes in the first place. Maximum red alert is when you're meeting new people or the going is rather sticky for some reason. Out of nervousness or desire to jolly things up you make some wild sweeping remark, you say something you don't really mean at all, and, clang, there it is and everybody is trying to skirt round it and the going is about twice as sticky as it was before.

Avoid:

- Age, weight, hair. (In fact, personal appearance in all aspects best left well alone. Worst disaster: 'When's the baby due?' to a non-pregnant woman.)
- All generalisations and dismissive remarks. (Somebody present is bound to be a Sunday footballer or a hair-dresser, to be rather fond of Bavarian dolls, to actually

drive a Mondeo or have personalised number plates . . . There's also the danger of looking racist, sexist, ageist, snobbish etc.)

- Food – never vent your dislikes *before* the meal.
- The catastrophe of saying, 'Lovely chicken,' when it was pork or, 'Lovely lamb,' when it was beef, by keeping compliments vague.
- Incriminating yourself. Have you remembered to put out all the ornaments and so forth that your guests have given you? Have you put away all invitations they might not have received?

Let's have a heated debate

Usually it's 'Let's not . . .'. The history of arguments at the table or in other social situations is a bloody one. The father of the travel writer, Robert Byron, once drove a fork into a daughter's thigh during an argument at lunch. Harold Pinter, visiting Balliol College in Oxford, was charm itself when he sat next to one of the few women dons in the college, Carol Clark, until, that is, he raised the subject of the Sandinistas, about whom he felt passionately. She did not disagree with him. She just said she knew nothing about them although she did know of certain similar movements in Africa. But this wasn't good enough. His manner changed so drastically towards her that she feared he was about to publicly denounce her.

Far from drawing us towards graciousness and elegance, social situations bring out the savage side. Top people are dragged down and in. Even Cecil Beaton, whose life was dedicated to substantial floral arrangements and the Queen Mother, got beaten up at an ambassador's party.

So we stalk amongst the crisps and nuts, tensed and alert for an attack, and, at the merest hint of danger, we take avoiding action. We change the subject, we say, 'I don't really care about fox-hunting,' or we make some flippant, deflecting remark: 'Quite frankly, I'd rather paint my nails.'

On top of this, the under thirties, the '*Big Brother*' generation, have a disturbingly laissez-faire attitude. 'Everyone's entitled to their opinion,' says Zoe. She sticks to this herself, unless someone says something nasty about dolphins.

The upshot of all this? Boredom. As Matt says, 'When my wife Lucy gets into a discussion about books it goes, "I've read this book," and the other person says, "Yes, so have I. Wasn't it fantastic? Now, have you read this other book?" They're just making a list really. It's a bit bland.'

So:

· Let's have more heated debate.

Don't be too quick to change the subject or make some deflating remark, to 'cut someone off at the knees'.

But there had better be some rules:

· It won't be fun if you're going to lose your temper *completely*, cry, or run away.
· It won't be fun if you're all going to shout at once.

- It won't be fun if you're going to utterly refuse to be reasonable at all costs.
- It won't be fun if you're going to bully those who are younger or less confident than you.

Don't worry if all these rules are thrown straight out of the window and half the guests end up in your under-stairs cupboard refusing to come out. This is a drama and people love it.

Talking about money – in one way or another

Hypocrisy abounds. Most people talk of little else while pretending not to. Matt and Lucy went on a mini-break to the Dordogne with another couple. Part of the point was no children, so it made sense to begin the day with extensive recollections of the havoc they create in the home. This led easily enough to rival estimates for steam cleaning all the carpets and upholstery (£500 upwards, thought very good), which allowed a thorough display of the extent of the home and its contents (number of lounges, bedrooms etc.); from there it was a short leap to the troublesome granite worktops (anything dropped smashed) versus the slate floor (even more unforgiving), the need to replace a Wedgwood dinner service (a bit eighties) . . . and so on throughout the day, leaving poor old Matt feeling not quite adequate. His kitchen doesn't have granite worktops. He looked at them, but they were too expensive.

Discussion of possessions is a sly but convenient way

of signalling your wealth. Everybody knows that granite worktops are expensive (even if thoroughly worth it). In Mrs Gibbs's day, this sort of talk was supposedly banned (although you wonder how many followed the rule). A duke once ordered a guest out of the house for *taking an interest* in the rather outstanding pictures. 'He was asking about a chap's things,' this duke spluttered.

This wasn't really democratic, a kind way of covering up differences of wealth and class. The underlying attitude was more 'mind your own business', 'don't be nosy'. Nowadays, driven on by our mania for labels and brands (in *Absolutely Fabulous*, Saffy anxiously asked her mother whether she liked the Christmas present she had just given her, to which Eddy replied that she liked it if it was Lacroix), our curiosity gets the better of us all the time. Just prices are enough. In January 2005, the Land Registry website went online, making it possible to find out definitively what people really paid for their properties. Instantly, it received half a million hits a day and made second billing on the Ten O'clock News. When we go round to other people's houses, we prod and poke and demand a 'guided tour'. We're terrifyingly explicit. 'Where did you get that?' 'What are those taps? Are they Hansgrohe? Is that sofa from the Conran Shop?' Matt is all too familiar with the situation. 'Somebody picked up a saucepan in our kitchen but she put it down again without a word when she saw it was Ikea.'

Sometimes, we just can't help ourselves, we find ourselves saying, 'Do you mind my asking . . . was it tremendously expensive?' or, more blastingly straightforward, 'Go on, spill the beans . . . how much?'

Talking about money is irresistible. Banning it would be disastrous. We'd live in a wasteland of silence. We all want to know how much they paid for the new bathroom, what their holiday cost, how much their house has gone up (or down). Coming away from their home, we'll speculate on how much they earn. Amazingly, for all her protestations to the contrary, not even Mrs Gibbs is immune. Why was she so eager to find out whether her grand neighbour, Lady Smiley, had travelled from London in first class?

But certain kinds of money talk and label talk (and behaviour) are insufferable – designed to diminish others or simply cruel. A woman I heard about said to a neighbour, 'I hear you're going to Mauritius. Now, look, you simply must take the helicopter from the airport to the Royal Palm – I assume you are staying at the Royal Palm – otherwise you'll see the most frightful poverty.' If you encounter this kind of thing, resist.

- Zoe met a young woman who complained that Hermès were dragging their feet about mending her handbag. 'It was a bit much *considering it cost £3,000.*' Zoe thought this was rather marvellous; it is unlikely anyone else would. It would have been better to say, 'But you can get a brilliant handbag from the Argos catalogue for only £7.99.'
- Be on the lookout for other underhand methods of mentioning the price. An ex-boyfriend of Zoe's, beginning to do well in advertising, bought an expensive leather jacket.

If it rains he makes a hysterical fuss, for apparently it will be ruined if it gets wet. He always takes the opportunity to add, 'It cost a bit, you know.' Someone should buy him a decent Pacamac from a street stall.

- Another horror is people saying, when a new job is in the offing, 'They're offering silly money.' This is false modesty and it's sick-making. A good response if you hear this is: 'Oh, yes. How much, exactly?'

- Any mention of what you earn, however indirect, is vulgar. Nor should you say to someone, 'I don't know how you can afford that on a teacher's salary,' or, 'I thought nurses only got about £20,000 a year.'

- The only exception is if someone is evidently very well paid; in that case, don't miss any opportunity for mockery: 'You must have more money than sense.' 'How much do you earn a second, would you say?' 'Do you charge for conversation?'

- Don't go around wrenching open people's jackets (while they are wearing them) to peer at the label. Not many would do this but Zoe's curiosity has got the better of her once or twice. Don't get caught inspecting the coats and so on in the bedroom either, unless you want to be mistaken for a thief or a pervert.

- Asking 'Is it Prada?' when it obviously isn't is just nasty.

On the other hand:

- There's nothing wrong with admiring people's possessions and clothes, asking where they came from, even how much they cost – but the one important exception is if there is someone present who might be made uncomfortable by it. In other words, someone who couldn't afford the kind of things you are talking about. But if there is someone who might afford much better things, on no account change the subject. Keep on about bargains at all costs (see **What if your friends are hugely richer than you?**, page 134).

- If you want this line of conversation, be prepared to accept the consequences. It's no good going into a sulk if you ask, 'What is it?' and they say, 'The usual,' meaning Prada. Don't let envy and competitiveness creep in.

- There's a lot to be said for a refreshingly bold approach. One couple say, 'How much was that coat?' 'What did you pay for your flat?' When this is met with a blank refusal to divulge, as it usually is, they say, 'We'll find out anyway.' And they do. This is so outrageous it has a certain charm.

- If you're asked, 'How much was it?' it is always appreciated if you add, either, 'I got 50 per cent off. It was the most wonderful bargain,' or, 'It's terrible. We'll be on the streets by the end of the month if we go on spending like this.' An uncompromising, matter-of-fact approach is fatal.

- Don't be strident and smug if someone asks about your Prada or your Dolce e Gabbana, but don't squirm with embarrassment either.

- If your Topshop skirt or Tesco trousers are admired and enquired into, don't be ashamed. Be proud. Matt was once hangdog about his M & S jacket. This is absurd. Your clothes are garnering compliments. What more do you want? In the 1980s, a launch party for one of Ivana Trump's novels was held in the Norman Hartnell salon. The publisher, Kate Parkin, was flattered that her dress was so much admired in such a place. Several journalists asked, 'What is it?' 'Asda,' she replied, adding shamelessly, 'It was £5.99.' The revelation grabbed the headlines.

Name-dropping

Somebody said to Norman St John-Stevas, now Lord St John Fawsley, 'You are such a name-dropper.' He replied, 'Funnily enough, the Queen was saying that to me only the other day.'

You've got to admit it, this is quite funny.

There was a dinner party once attended by rivalrous gentlemen, one camp from the TV world, the other from the world of books. Competitive name-dropping broke out. One of the TV people had actually met President Reagan, who had proudly told him of his advice to the distinguished Oxbridge-educated prime minister of a Caribbean island: 'When I was a boy in Illinois, we found a carburettor and an axle and we built a car with our bare hands. Now that's what you folks want to be doing here.' But this was only the beginning. Later there was to be Claudette Colbert and finally, would you believe, Mrs Onassis. One of the other TV people described how he had encountered a vaguely familiar tall woman at a party, unrecognised until Edna O'Brien, standing by, enquired, in her Irish lilt, 'Do y'know Mrs Onassis?' – marvellous. Only the most famous woman in the world. The grandeur of it. All the book side could lob back with was dreary old Iris Murdoch and other cardiganed lady authors.

Everybody there agreed they wouldn't have missed it for the world.

Otherwise there's: 'Nelson – Nelson Mandela – was just saying to me yesterday . . .' 'You mean you know him?' 'Yes, I do actually.' Or 'I told that story at lunch last week and Kylie nearly dropped off her seat.' We've come across this before. This is name-dropping in its purest form (see **More than one name – Nicknames and the in-crowd question**, page 142), where it is ideal to refer to the person by a nickname or familiar name. Often name-droppers let themselves down by getting these wrong: 'I'd better get a move on. Can't keep Madge waiting.' Well, actually, Madge is what the tabloids call Madonna. Apparently she loathes it (it would be surprising if a person didn't loathe being called Madge). Sometimes it is desperate. Someone I know wrote to their old school magazine to sum up their life: 'I was greeted in the bar at Covent Garden by Herbert von Karajan and a laureate once said hello to me.'

This kind of name-dropping is boring, pointless and rude. The dropper is trying to gain stature and make others feel small but they end up looking absurd. The whole thing's usually a pack of lies, in any case.

- Don't hesitate if you've got a good story about a well-known person, provided it's got *something* to do with the conversation. These titbits are often the highlight of a social occasion. But some modesty is called for. 'Do you actually know Barry Manilow?' 'Well, just a little . . . not really.'
- Tiresome name-droppers deserve a good blasting counter-attack (see **More than one name – Nicknames and the in-crowd question**, page 142).

Hideous embarrassments

Completely and utterly appallingly embarrassing situations occur rarely but when they do they are shattering and never forgotten.

'The most embarrassing thing that happened to me *ever*,' says Matt (this must be serious when there have been so many) 'was when I met someone socially who'd turned me down for a job. He said, "I didn't interview you for a job, did I?" in this horrible patronising way and I just said, "No, it must have been someone else." But I think we both knew it wasn't true and I felt about this high. We avoided each other for the rest of the evening.'

Or, as Zoe did, you might meet someone whose car you've crashed into (she just said, 'I crashed into your car, didn't I?' and giggled helplessly), or who you nearly ran over . . . How about: one of the other guests turns out to be the person you've just been in a road-rage incident with outside in the street!

- Nothing will do but immense boldness. If you're going to hide away, it's hopeless.
- The ball is certainly in the court of the turner-down, the runner-over, the one who caused the car crash, the one who lost their temper first in the road-rage incident. You have to say, 'I'm sorry we couldn't give you the job.' Or, 'It was a very difficult decision.' Or, 'It's always something of a lottery, isn't it?' Or, 'I'm sorry I crashed into your car. It was entirely my fault,' and so on. They're feeble old clichés *but they work* because they convey a kind intention.
- The 'victims' should be gracious.
- There should be an effort at further conversation.

Networking

Mrs Gibbs recalls her mother, at a party in the 1930s, chatting perfectly amiably with someone called the Honourable Mrs Treby. But when Lord Meavy came into the room, some hidden machinery in her chair appeared to catapult this Honourable across the room towards the Lord, leaving Mrs Gibbs Senior high and dry.

Networking is nothing new. But today we see more of the commercial kind. People like Zoe, who is in PR, view every social occasion, regardless of who might be there, as an opportunity to tout for business and build up 'contacts'. Matt tells of a 'really bum evening with this guy completely dominating the conversation, because he was involved in launching a thing called In For U which was a sort of socket you'd have on the outside of your house where all the stuff you'd ordered on the Internet could be delivered. The idea was you didn't have to wait in for a delivery. He seemed to think it was a bloody amazing idea. He said the supermarkets were interested. This was quite a few years ago. I haven't heard of it catching on, have you?'

Social networking is just social climbing. Zoe would love to go in for it, if she got the chance. She's longing to meet Jonathan Ross and she reads *Hello!* magazine with a magnifying glass every week. Her tendency to glance around to see if there isn't someone more important to talk to could well get out of control.

- Networking is selfish.
- Social networking doesn't work. Normal people see straight through social networkers and so do top people (one of the reasons why they're top). The best networkers can hope for is to be taken on as some kind of desperate groupie (even a sex slave, as has been known).
- How to fight the networkers – pull the carpet out from under. Be mean, be sarcastic. 'Look, you must talk to that person over there. She does Martine McCutcheon's toenails.' Or, 'That one – she's in charge of keeping the moth out of Madonna's winter knits.' Or, 'She's Victoria Wood's ex-sister-in-law. I think you'd get on so well.'

Some kinds of networking may be unavoidable and not necessarily harmful.

- Someone you meet at a party might turn out to be 'useful' to you in your professional life. If you both establish there and then a mutual interest and agree to take it further, this is straightforward – but make sure this is done discreetly, without the other guests being bothered.
- If the other person needs to be 'pushed', this absolutely must be left to a subsequent occasion. If you can't wait, your pushing will get you nowhere, except into disgrace. It is terribly unfair on the other person, who was looking forward to some harmless relaxation, and it is highly likely that the other guests will get dragged into it all somehow or other.
- If you find yourself being pushed, be firm. Say, 'We'll talk about this later, perhaps. Now, what's your favourite seaside resort?'
- If it only occurs to you to pursue the 'contact' after the occasion is over, this should be done through the hosts who brought you together in the first place. If you approach directly, you are imposing and reduce your chances of getting anywhere. Your hosts can find out if your approaches would be welcome. Matt and Lucy were once alarmed to discover that one of their guests, who owned a discount bookstore, had taken to ferociously phoning up another, a publisher, to try and wrest cheap books out of her.

Speaking and Language Manners

'Now I will just say a few words'

Richard Ingrams thinks this the 'most disagreeable combi-
nation of words in the English language'. For Kingsley Amis,
it was 'red or white?'

Speech making at private social occasions has proliferated
vastly in recent years. The feeling is that no birthday party,
wedding anniversary, house-warming party, house-closing
party is complete without a speech.

Matt went to a wedding where the best man, who was a
friend of his, launched as usual on a speech. He described
his first encounter with the bride, when he did not see her
but heard her screams of sexual ecstasy through the thin
partition wall in the flat he shared with the groom, but
there was nothing unusual about this because his mate, the
groom, was always going out to bars and pulling birds,
although this one did appear to be more into it than some
of the others . . .

The upshot of all this is that, now, the best man is barred

from ever entering the marital home and if the groom wishes to see him he has to do so elsewhere.

It is a reasonable assumption (who cares about proper research?) that at least three quarters of all speeches are disastrous, but in different ways.

- If you are preparing to make a speech, the first thing to grasp is that nobody wants to hear it. Speeches interrupt the fun. The guests have to be quiet and listen – usually to frightful rubbish. The spectre of hideous embarrassment hangs over them.
- It should be short, short, short. Two and a half minutes is too long.
- Whatever you prepare, cut it in half.
- Never launch into the history of anything or anybody. No matter how brilliant you are, people will be thinking, 'He's still only got to 1948.'
- Keep thanks to the absolute minimum. Your guests will be seething with resentment if the list of flower arrangers or childminders and other people they've never heard of goes on interminably.
- Keep soul baring and all embarrassing gush out of it.
- Anything risqué or even faintly unflattering should be thought about very carefully in advance. Look what happened to Matt's friend. One of Mrs Gibbs's friends was put out by the speech at her eightieth-birthday party which went, 'You're a difficult old girl but your bark's not as bad as your bite.'
- Speeches should be true but appropriate.

- If someone says, 'I love making speeches,' never ask them to make a speech. They will be a vain windbag who never prepares or takes advice. They ramble on. Their speech will be a total catastrophe.
- The best speeches are made by people eaten up with nerves who want to sit down as quickly as possible.

'Speech! Speech!' It's terrible when people are forced to make a speech, sometimes in reply to one that has been made about them. A horrible baying cry goes up, 'Speech! Speech!' Where does such savagery come from (see **Strippograms**, page 180 and **Surprise parties**, page 182)? 'I did say I wouldn't go if there were going to be speeches,' says Mrs Gibbs of her own eightieth-birthday party, 'but my nephew insisted on a short one and he had the sense to say that I wouldn't reply. Even so, a few people started baying for blood but I wasn't having it.'

- Anyone tormented by 'Speech! Speech!' must absolutely refuse to speak on principle.

Do I speak nicely?

Or 'naycely' perhaps it should be? Pronunciation, vocabulary and grammar – anxieties about these are to do with class and education, not manners. Despite everybody always saying, 'It's a classless society,' and, 'Down with snobbery,' it's astonishing how much people worry about the way they speak – although they would never admit it, of course. Even

Zoe is a little thrown if she meets someone who says 'loo' and not 'toilet'. There is a split-second delay while she decides whether or not to switch. In *Big Brother 5* Dan, who came from the north, would always hesitantly correct himself if he said 'tea' instead of 'dinner'. The other day, Matt said 'bollyvard' by mistake when he was talking to his rich friend who, as luck would have it, is half French. 'I felt a complete idiot. But he was very charming about it. He took a lot of trouble to avoid the word afterwards. He started saying, "those large streets".'

- Who cares if you say 'toilet' or 'loo', 'napkin' or 'serviette', 'lounge' or 'sitting room'? If they do, that's their problem.
- Suit yourself and don't apologise.
- But others may not be as liberated as you. If you meet someone who says 'sitting room' and you say 'lounge', you follow suit, you chime in. So if they say 'sitting room' before you've had a chance to get in with 'lounge', then 'sitting room' it is.
- An alternative is to avoid mentioning the word altogether. When you know people better you can be more open about your differences.
- If someone mispronounces a word, even a foreign word, or says it differently from how you would, on no account correct them either directly or, worst of all, by implication (i.e. by saying it in your way with menacing emphasis). You say the word in the same way as them or not at all. Mrs Gibbs's mother had some friends who always said 'med-er-ve-al' instead of 'medi-evil'. So she was con-

demned through all her life to remembering to say 'Med-er-ve-al' when they were about – how kind old manners were from time to time!

- If someone speaks ungrammatically (not the odd lapse but consistently so), this can be ignored. You speak in your way and they in theirs.

Bad language

Mrs Whitehouse insisted that bad language on TV would lead to the breakdown of society.

But it hasn't. It hasn't even led to an increase in bad language – except on TV and amongst children. There is rather a lot of swearing on the streets, but that is a different matter.

Matt's children know not to swear or use bad language in front of adults, although nobody has ever told them specifically not to. Their language amongst themselves would probably beggar belief, but nobody has ever heard it. Very young children sometimes swear at the wrong moment, but this just throws the parents into a dubious light. At a family funeral, the two-year-old daughter of the novelist Sarah Long, screamed, 'Where are my fucking crayons?' (It's all right to swear in print, by the way.) 'Where did she get that from?' the rows of strict Baptist aunts were evidently thinking.

Even dedicated swearers seem to be able to restrain themselves in the presence of royalty except for one eccentric nightclub owner who, during the war, found *four* kings in exile (this really is true) seeking entry. 'Get a table for these fucking kings,' he bellowed to the waiter.

You might think that little has changed since Eliza Doolittle caused outrage by bellowing, 'Move your bleeding arse!' at Royal Ascot nearly a hundred years ago. But the continued unpopularity of bad language at social occasions has little to do with stuffy adherence to tradition and more to do with a desire not to come across as irritable or angry or inarticulate and boring.

It isn't so clear what to do if you want to tell a funny story of which bad language is an essential part – usually the punch-line. Matt once got into hot water with his story of the vicar who developed Tourette's syndrome and announced from the pulpit, 'May the Lord fucking bless you,' or perhaps it was, 'May the fucking Lord bless you.' This didn't go down well when he and Lucy invited the new neighbours round – they seemed up for this kind of thing but turned out to have an ardent Christian side.

- Don't swear at social occasions. It's just not nice.
- Stories with swearing as a feature might go down all right, but judge your audience very carefully.
- Swear to your heart's content within the bosom of your family and with your intimate friends – although don't forget that a little *variety* of vocabulary is always attractive.
- Older people sometimes like to slip a few swear-words into their conversation or tell a risqué story to show that they are up to date. This is perfectly all right. Mrs Gibbs's

set piece is about how her nephew, as a child of five, saw the farmer coming across the field and said, 'He's a bugger, isn't he?' She and her sister had to fight not to drop their cups of tea (they didn't want the boy to know they were convulsed with laughter). But, just because an older person uses a swear-word, it does *not* mean everybody else can.

Rude stories

· As with swearing, these are best kept for your closest friends. People you don't know so well might be embarrassed, less by the content, more by the assumption of greater intimacy than is in fact the case.

Special Manners for Special Occasions

Surviving the stand-up party

Of course, you can have fun, but let's be honest – modern informality has turned the stand-up party into wild, lawless bandit country. The most spectacular outrages may occur where the under thirties are involved, but no age group is immune, not even Mrs Gibbs's. 'I was talking to a woman I didn't know at a drinks party recently when one of her friends barged into the conversation. Before I knew it they were off talking about some holiday they were planning together and I was frozen out completely.'

At the gathering after Gianni Versace's funeral in Milan, even Princess Diana was left standing on her own. Alexandra Shulman, editor of *Vogue*, who was present, commented, 'Even the most famous woman in the world could find herself stranded with nobody to talk to at a social occasion.'

And this is just the tip of the iceberg – at the stand-up party you don't just get people being ignored or interrupted.

You can have pushing and shoving, conversations abruptly terminated as people ineptly 'move on', no smiling, people met earlier nuked with a blank stare, drunkenness, fights, the wrong people flirting with the wrong people, dangerous spontaneous outbreaks of sex.

No, this won't do at all. Something must be done at once, to protect the shy and the vulnerable as much as anything else.

A few simple adjustments should make the world of difference:

- First and foremost, if you see someone standing on their own, treat it as an emergency, like a fire or something. Take immediate action. There should be no wallflowers. At a good party, there never are.

- By the same token, if someone is hovering near your group, don't keep them waiting for ages and ages before you condescend to speak. In fact, try not to keep them waiting at all (although they clearly don't expect you to break off your conversation immediately, which is why they are hovering politely). Matt suffers terribly in this respect: 'You wait about and they just turn their backs towards you that little bit more.'

- Don't interrupt. I hope that sounds sufficiently severe. I'll say it again: Don't interrupt. The classic scenario is that endured by Mrs Gibbs – you see an old friend talking to someone you've never seen in your life before. You can't help yourself. As far as you are concerned, this new person just isn't there. You interrupt. You probably ignore the stranger. You have arrived equipped with your own conversation. You may not mean any harm, but you might as well be a tornado or an earthquake as far as that other conversation is concerned. Anxiety that your friend will be upset if you don't say hello straight away is no excuse. That can wait for an appropriate moment when you can greet each other properly.

- If you are interrupting to say goodbye, you are on firmer ground. But always apologise to those you interrupt and keep your farewells brief.

- Interrupters in general are the bane of modern social life (see **Interrupting**, page 149).

- If you want to get past, ask. There is a horrible new practice of 'moving' people out of the way by putting both hands on either someone's shoulders or their sides. Alternative procedures for people who have forgotten their manners are traditional pushing, as practised by schoolchildren, or drilling one finger into the back or arm. Touching people you don't know, even with the best of intentions, is a highly sensitive issue nowadays and is best avoided altogether. If you really can't attract the person's attention (stand-up parties can be noisy and people can be engrossed in conversation), then the lightest touch on the arm should be enough. Any show of impatience will be properly resented (see also **Where to begin? 'Good morning,' 'Thank you,' pushing and shoving – among other things**, page 7).

- On the other hand, always be alert to the possibility that *you* might be in the way. Don't drape yourself seductively all over the banisters, blocking the route to the loo.

• *Always* smile at or acknowledge other guests, even if you don't talk to them. Otherwise, you might as well spend the evening milling about at a railway station. Come along! You may be shy, but it is supposed to be a party.

If we can get all this right, we'll be getting somewhere.

What are hosts supposed to do at the stand-up party?

If Zoe gives a party her duties end with the provision of a venue and a certain amount of food and drink. Beyond that, guests can fend for themselves. Matt is the opposite. He finds giving a big party traumatic. After the last one, it is doubtful he will give another in his life. He becomes fraught, rushing round, jamming people together, hoovering up the wallflowers. It is rather pitiable.

Hosts have a subtle and all-pervasive effect that is not often remarked on. Guests unconsciously take their cue from them. If the hosts are taciturn, unwelcoming, offhand, then the guests will be too. And it works the other way. If hosts are friendly, kind, whacky, lunatic . . .

• So, hosts, especially younger ones, make a point of greeting your guests in the way you want the party to go on.

Make sure they have their first drink and somebody to talk to. After that, do your best to fill up the odd glass, help out people with no one to talk to and so on, without driving yourself completely round the bend. Remember that you can't be responsible for everything.

- You will feel more relaxed if you have done a certain amount of organising beforehand. If guests are to help themselves to drinks and food, make sure this can happen without a jam. It's easy to underestimate how much of a jam only a few people will create.

- If possible, get help. Commandeer children or close friends. Don't be put off hiring help. This is often a real bargain and agencies have a lot of students on their books who are massively competent and talk amongst themselves (when there's a moment) about quarks or how the futures market works.

Introducing at the stand-up party

Be careful about introducing. Matt laments that he is often dragged away, by a well-meaning host, from an enjoyable conversation about football to meet someone who works in trade magazines like he does. 'I don't really want to talk about trade magazines on a Saturday night and usually the other person doesn't want to, either. Anyway, I'm on the money side of it.'

- There may be a very good reason for introducing people but similar work, interests or personality often isn't one (see **Who to invite?**, page 56). A stand-up party perhaps is not the best occasion for introductions. It is best to avoid breaking up ongoing, perfectly viable conversations (so it can be near impossible to find a moment when both parties are 'free') and it is also important to gauge whether the person really wants to be introduced. It should not be forced on them. This can be tricky to establish at a busy party.

- On the whole, hosts should only introduce people at parties who appear to have no one to talk to or who look as though they are stuck with someone. In this case it is reasonable to impose on an existing group.

Moving on at the stand-up party

This is one of the major disaster zones of modern manners. How do you end a conversation at a party and move on? Only for Mrs Gibbs is it straightforward: 'You just say, "Would you excuse me, I really must talk to so-and-so . . .".'

But for younger people, this is too formal. What do we have to replace it? Nothing. Matt is traumatised, Zoe traumatises others. 'I really really hate it,' says Matt. Sometimes he resorts to the transparent subterfuge of, 'I'm just going to get another drink,' before slinking away. 'Sometimes I try something else, like, "It's been nice talking to you," but it's just all so embarrassing and I know they'll think I'm shifty and insincere.' Another low tactic, a great favourite with Zoe, is to wait until a third person joins the conversation and then use them as cover for a quick, silent getaway.

None of this will do at all – unless you want to create the impression that you have been bored by the person you've been talking to. Why else all this dodgy, guilty carry-on?

We really are completely at sea.

- Don't say, 'I'm just going to get another drink.'
- Don't make a silent getaway when another person joins your conversation.
- You've got to say *something*.
- Some therapy. Get rid of all this guilt. It's perfectly natural to want to move on. All conversations, however enjoyable, have got to end some time.
- Remove the guilt and you will feel more confident about dealing with the situation graciously – and you'll be more convincing too. It doesn't matter which of the standard forms you choose: 'It's been nice meeting you,' or 'I've enjoyed talking to you.' Just be robust and straight-forward.

Saying goodbye at the stand-up party

Confusion reigns as usual. Even Zoe knows that you should say goodbye to the hosts, but she doesn't bother with anyone else. Matt worries. What if there are two hosts? What about the people you've spoken to at the party? 'Lucy usually has the party all over again, going round saying goodbye to *everybody* while I wait by the door.'

- Where there are two hosts, don't be idle. Seek them both out. You can interrupt conversations to say goodbye but be brief.
- Hosts, be on the lookout for guests wanting to say goodbye and try not to keep them waiting. Usually, once people have decided to leave, they become rather single-minded about it.
- Say goodbye to people you've met at the party *who happen to be about* when you are leaving. Otherwise, they will think that you wish you'd never met them.

Strippograms

Marriages have foundered, couples have split up, friends have fallen out for good, because some twit has taken it upon themselves to order a strippogram as a lovely surprise, usually for a birthday party. Women especially hate it, however much they may feel bullied into whooping and screaming with delight. Even Zoe, can you imagine, was appalled when one was inflicted on her on her twenty-fifth birthday.

'It wasn't harmless fun. I felt like I was being made to perform some weird kind of sex act in front of all my friends.' Afterwards, there was all hell to pay. She launched a Scotland-Yard-style inquiry to find out who had done it.

Where did the idea come from that the perfect way to treat people who are at the centre of a social occasion is to humiliate and mock them?

- Strippograms are completely and utterly ghastly and nobody should have anything to do with them, ever.
- Surprise strippograms aren't on in what might appear more promising situations either – in all-male or all-female company, for instance. If people want to go to strip clubs or look at porn, they're welcome, but this type of entertainment should not be compulsory.
- Here's what you do if you find yourself subject to a strippogram. Make a scene. Stand up and assume perfect poise. Look imperious but just this side of utterly terrifying. Say, 'There must be some mistake. Let's see if we can find you some clothes.' Take the strippogram by the arm, approach the person most likely to be responsible for the outrage and suggest that that person surrenders at least a jacket or maybe even a pair of trousers to the unfortunate strippogram. Keep up the pretence that it's all in the best of humour and really they'd be a spoilsport to refuse. It might just work.

Surprise parties

Do you have to?

If you're planning such a thing, examine your motives. Are you sure you're not being just a tiny bit sadistic? We want to make a fuss of people and celebrate them but lurking below the surface is unconscious resentment. So he thinks he's special just because he's turned sixty, does he? Let's knock him down a peg or two. Watch out that the savage impulse isn't getting the better of you!

Surprise parties are in the same category as strippograms and speeches extorted from the unprepared. They are unwelcome because the victim is cornered and has no choice.

Mrs Gibbs says, 'My nephew was planning a surprise party for my seventieth birthday. But when he rang up my friends they all threw up their hands in horror and said they couldn't think of anything more dreadful and it must be stopped at once. He was intending to invite all sorts of unsuitable people. I wouldn't have known where to look. Thank goodness it never happened.'

If you insist on a surprise party, the following will almost certainly happen:

- The person will find out about it anyway.
- The person will burst into tears on arrival and continue sobbing throughout.
- The person will die from the shock (this has indeed happened).

- The person would have worn a different outfit if they'd known about it.
- The person would have invited entirely different people if they'd known about it.
- The person will fail to recognise various old friends and acquaintances.
- The person will feel disoriented and confused throughout.

Extreme Manners

Crisis situations: When they've just got to go – or have they?

Bad behaviour on social occasions can be fun. There was a time when Zoe acquired a rich and somewhat older boyfriend. She was required to produce a bridge supper; as far as she was concerned a totally alien thing. She got appallingly drunk and boiled some globe artichokes for thirty seconds when what they need is forty minutes. But it made a good story – the solemn and polite bridge four trying to eat the raw leathery leaves.

But the following cannot be put up with and must be removed from the scene at once. If there is only a hostess, as many able-bodied male guests as possible should assist, although it could be that if she is an international bodybuilder or something of that kind and a show of strength is called for, she will be able to manage quite well on her own. The categories are:

- Drunks, especially if they are likely to be sick or steal all the children's shoes.
- People bruising for a fight, or actually having one.
- People who've taken so many drugs they don't know who or where they are and keep on falling over (largely because they are in the way).

If guests are merely disgustingly rude or start leering at your wife, you just have to endure this. It's your fault for asking them; you'll have to wait until afterwards to make a scene. Once an invitation has been given, it cannot be taken back. It is a matter of honour.

- In the old days, horrible grand people used to get rid of unwanted guests by making the butler inform them that their bags had been packed. Even if you do it yourself, asking guests to leave or disinviting them, however justified, will always seem a lordly act. It is best avoided. It will also have a demoralising effect on your other friends. They'll all start wondering when their turn will be. It's pointless complaining that such anxiety is irrational – it's as inevitable as the guilt experienced by the blameless going through customs.

Sex, Filth and Couples Manners

Chatting up, dating, turning down

If you start chatting someone up, if they like you, if you get along, how it all progresses (or doesn't) might not be straightforward but it hasn't got much to do with manners. You might make the mistake, as Matt did in his dating days, of virtually taking out a mortgage on the first marital home within five minutes of meeting someone. Or you might, like certain of Zoe's male friends, blunder with premature references to underwear from Agent Provocateur. But it's just possible that these might not be mistakes. When Matt eventually met Lucy they were engaged within the month and mortgaged within the year. Similarly, some of these cool young men have had a certain amount of success with their sexy talk. You do hear of the most extraordinary things.

If you go on a date, the only mistake might be too many manners – all trussed up in your Sunday best, behaving perfectly. It's ghastly.

• Let's not have too many manners in intimate situations!

But what happens if they don't like you? This is where manners come in. When were you last turned down nicely? Ineptitude about saying no is endemic. Is it just embarrassment, or arrogance, or the strange belief that it's all the other person's fault – they've put me on the spot, they're after me, so I can behave how I like?

Which is worse? The cowards who offer to buy or get you a drink, then vanish, or give you a bogus telephone number ('the number you have dialled has not been recognised')? The strong silent types who blank you completely, or the primitive grunting ones who make grudging monosyllabic replies? What about the really thrusting cool cats, who say bluntly, 'Look, I'm just not interested,' or, if you offer to buy them a drink, 'No, but can I have the money?' Or there's the cruel reverse of this, as it were: 'Would you like a drink?' 'Oh, yes, please.' 'They're over there.'

Nobody ever forgets an unkind rejection. People will be discouraged from trying again if they get a curt brush-off. They may even develop a stand-offish way themselves, out of defensiveness. Before we know it, everybody will be doing it, and then we'll have the surreal situation of parties, bars and clubs full of people refusing to speak.

• It's a social responsibility, as well as a kindness, to try to turn someone down nicely.
• Don't fall for the give-them-an-inch-and-they'll-take-a-mile school of thought. Exchanging a few words doesn't

mean that you're going to be dragged straight away into some grotesque sex scene. To refuse to speak or to be systematically stand-offish is actually just rather horrible. Some people will be incited to taunts and mockery.

- Besides, if you talk to them a little, there's always the hope that they will decide they're not so keen after all.

- Much will depend on your tone of voice. It's not so difficult to be reserved and rather distant without being impolite.

- The crunch will inevitably come when you are being asked to go further than you want. Maybe it is an offer to buy or get you a drink or something rather more direct. It may seem absurd, but why should these invitations not be treated as any other (see **Saying no nicely**, page 80). In other words, it is nice to be asked, but no thank you very much. This will also be a good opportunity to end the encounter. Be decisive. Don't say, 'See you later,' or, 'Maybe see you again,' because this will be taken as encouragement. 'Goodbye. I'd better be moving on now,' will do.

- If you see the poor rejected person later, it's not absolutely necessary to ignore them.

- Of course, sometimes people are just too pushy, even bullying. They won't go away. You could try a therapeutic approach, patiently explaining that these methods are never going to work. If that gets you nowhere, then, sadly, you will have to take more drastic action.

- Straight men and women are not to get in a huff if cruised by gay men and women. They should be flattered – and often are, if the truth be told. Try to take a metrosexual approach. It's very modern. Matt once had a man coming on to him. 'I tried to explain that I wasn't exactly . . . sort of . . . available . . . wife and kids and all that . . . and he said he hadn't ever been turned down so nicely.' Well done! So you got that one right, Matt.

Couples on their best behaviour

At a party recently, Zoe's current boyfriend behaved very badly. He seemed to be coming on to another girl. When Zoe tried to prise him away, he said pointedly that he was having a very interesting conversation about demographics and why didn't she make herself scarce? She and her girl-friends must have masses more to say about *I'm a Celebrity, Get Me out of Here*. Zoe made a scene, and soon the other girl, the other girl's boyfriend and, in fact, most of the other guests were piling in. It ended up with the person who was giving the party in tears, wishing they'd *all* go away.

If there are not alarming scenes, there is often persistent bickering. 'You're sitting on the ironing.' 'That's not how you peel a sprout.' 'You know I don't like it this cold.' 'Why have you thrown the paper away already?'

But perhaps couples getting along beautifully, hosing each other down with syrup, cooing and simpering is the worst.

- Couples, when with others, behave.
- If a serious scene is brewing, get away. Have it in private.
- If your partner is making you jealous, for whatever

reason, you have to be terribly noble, self-sacrificing and brave. Don't spoil it for everyone else. If it's too distressing, leave on your own. This is probably the best way of bringing your silly partner to heel anyway.

· Don't kiss and coo and sweet-talk in front of others to excess. You'll be cruelly mocked as soon as your back is turned. And it's not as if everyone else can join in, is it?

Filth

Raunchy e-mails, dirty text messages – what have they got to do with manners? Well, a lot of them get sent, with, allegedly, David Beckham leading the way. Of course, as long as they remain private, manners don't come into it. But often they don't, as was seen most spectacularly in the year 2000 when Bradley Chait of the City law firm Norton Rose sent an innocent e-mail to some mates boasting rather too graphically of his girlfriend's enjoyment of oral sex. Within hours, due to one of these mates feeling 'honour-bound to circulate' the message, which led to an astonishing mania to 'find this girl' (the particular compliment being, apparently, remarkably rare), one million people all over the world had read this message and were reduced to a state of frantic sexual frenzy. According to the *Daily Mail*, the worst humiliation was for the girl's parents, who lived in a nice manor house somewhere.

But was it such a humiliation?

During the Beckham affair, a few middle-aged lady journalists tried to make out that it was all a bit sick. But everybody else followed the example of the French who were ecstatic about the whole thing: '*Quel homme!*' their headlines declared.

- So feel free to carry on transmitting filth to your heart's content.
- There is just one little complication. You can send sexy messages and a lot of people might know about it but don't get carried away. It isn't on to actually talk like that in a social situation. That would be a mistake. You'll be met with bored indifference. Even on *Big Brother 5*, where you'd have thought exhibitionists would abound, Victor's attempts at outrageous sexual discussion were a disaster. 'Have you ever done anything really pervy?' he said. There was a silence. Eventually someone said, 'Like what?' in a weary way. That was the end of that.

Body-hair manners

The American-porn-star look for men – i.e. muscles and no chest hair, the effect peculiar, like an inflatable doll – is no longer in. But no nicely brought-up man has hair on his shoulders or back. Some gyms provide hair-removal services and many waxing establishments cater for men these days as well. If you don't get rid of it yourself, you can be sure someone else will.

Substance Manners

Smoking

Zoe won't have it at all. Smokers are put out in her sour Balham back garden with the neighbours' cats. The wife of a well-known pianist has the same policy, although this lady is more erratic, going along with smoking for a time, then suddenly turfing out. Matt dithers about, looking for ash-trays just a little grudgingly. At one time he operated some-thing called a 'no-smoking policy' in his home. All the smokers Mrs Gibbs knows are dead.

Health aside, the manners of smoking are easy:

- Guests should always ask if they may and hosts should always say yes.
- Try not to ask, as many do, with the cigarette already in your mouth and the lighter poised.
- In some homes you may get a strong sense that smoking won't be welcome (Cancer Research collecting tins in the hall, hosts known to be in training for the London

Marathon), in which case it would be best not to ask at all.

- Once you've got permission, don't get carried away. Look to see how other guests are reacting. Certainly don't smoke while others are eating or in between courses (this really is about the worst thing you can do).
- Hosts, don't be prissy. Unless smoking is actually going to kill you there and then (or you have asthma), it's inhospitable to insist that people go outside. A bit of smoking in the home isn't going to mean that you'll have to redecorate and send all your soft furnishings to the cleaners.

Matt's 'no-smoking policy' (he never actually had notices pinned up) came to a sad end when he and Lucy made the mistake of giving a small celebration for his younger sister who had won a hairdressing award. She was allowed to invite her own friends. The result was that a great gang of smokers got in and couldn't be stopped.

Drugs

Suppose you go round to some people for the evening. Everything is perfectly normal – Jamie Oliver salady sort of starter, a bit of salmon next, Ikea cutlery. Then afterwards, you're in the sitting room, and before you know it, instead of Tia Maria or Milk Tray, drugs are being offered. Or perhaps *as well as* these homely delights. What do you do? Rise grandly to your feet, declare, 'I didn't realise I'd been invited to a drug den,' and storm out? Would this be right?

Matt has been in this situation not a few times. Once he was tempted to join in – out of politeness. But on the whole he is rather law-abiding. Another time, he says, 'I was a bit surprised when they first produced the stuff. Up until then, it had been decidedly upmarket – Nigella and the Conran Shop. This little mucky parcel wrapped up in old clingfilm didn't fit in at all.' He was uncomfortable, of course, if not a little panic-stricken. But it wasn't long before the whole evening started to roll quietly downhill. 'It was just so boring. They all started to sound like the record had slowed down. One of them kept trying to tell me something about a table. I'm not sure if it was one that was in the room or another one. "This table ... it's just so ... it's a table ... it's so ... intense." Then he'd say, "You don't get it, do you?" After a while, he'd start up again: "This table ...".' Quentin Crisp, speaking of drugged-up guests at non-drug parties, put it well: 'Since most people cannot tell the difference between natural and chemically induced stupidity you are likely to pass yourself off as a dull but happy fellow.'

- No need to make a scene by leaving the minute drugs are produced. A police visit is unlikely (although, in London, you might be slightly afraid of the new Metropolitan Police Commissioner's bold threat to raid dinner parties and stamp out middle-class drug abuse). If you don't want to join in, you won't have to wait long before the hosts are so out of it that you can get away without the slightest risk of giving offence. Why not enjoy the benefit of a nice early night?

- Drug users, in social situations, don't insist on everybody participating. The idea is, 'All the more for us.'
- Hosts, before they rocket off to drug heaven, should ensure that a certain amount of discretion is being observed – that drugs are not being consumed in view of the street and so on. (Remember, this is a book of manners, not a manual on how to dodge the filth.)

I don't want to get Zoe into trouble, but her interest in marijuana doesn't always go down so well. Some people think she rather overdoes it. Although she always asks if she may, this isn't a good idea in the first place if you're round at the flat shared by some pompous young lawyers you don't know too well, who have just been warned by the senior partner that even the tiniest criminal offence will wreck their careers.

- At small parties, don't ask if you may take drugs unless you are very sure of your ground. Since drug takers, like children, always share their sweets (although nobody makes them; they just do), drugs could very quickly come to dominate the occasion.
- It is normally the hosts' privilege to initiate drug taking.
- Unless it is obviously a druggy scene, don't ask to take drugs (or just start doing it) at a large party.
- If you are an addict, there is little that manners can do for you.

If you are interested, amongst themselves drug takers exhibit perfect manners. There is a complicated etiquette which ensures that everybody takes their turn to supply the drugs. Once they are on the table, as it were, drugs are always shared and anyone hogging more than their fair share is despised in the same way as someone who fails to buy their round in the pub.

Condolence Manners

Offering condolences

How many of us wish we had done more condoling when younger? Matt does. Zoe, in common with many young people, if she thinks about it at all, assumes that her mother will do it for her, when remoter members of the family die. She remains silent. As did Matt, some years ago, when his step-aunt's mother died. She was well over eighty and had been thrown out of every old people's home in the neighbourhood on account of her bad language and habit of very properly attacking garden gnomes. Her last years had been difficult. But after nine months of inertia, Matt suddenly decided to send a letter of condolence to the step-aunt. Fortunately, in this case the aunt merely thought it bizarre. 'Has he only just heard?' she enquired of Matt's mother.

Matt has tried his best, but it hasn't been easy. Another time, he met one of Lucy's friends at a party, some weeks after her mother had died. He offered condolences. There were other people around who hadn't heard. They were very concerned. 'It all developed into quite a thing and Lucy's friend was quite upset.'

Then there's all the worry about what to say. Nobody wants to be the person who, unconcerned by the main event, the assassination of her husband at the theatre, asked, 'But what did you think of the play, Mrs Lincoln?' Should you be euphemistic? Is it bad form to use the dread words, 'dead', 'died', 'death'? Should you behave rather like a professional mourner, as it were rending your clothes and gnashing your teeth? Or should you try to be jaunty, cheerful, even tell a few jokes?

- You can't send too many letters of condolence. They are always appreciated. Don't forget the remoter members of the family. Don't forget grandchildren and children, who are often overlooked if there is a widow or widower or parent remaining. Close friends, also, might not be thought of.
- You can send a general letter of condolence, addressed, say, to a widow and all her children.
- Don't dither with your condolences. They do need to be offered straight away, either by letter or in person. A delay could be upsetting. When people begin to recover from a bereavement they may not want to be reminded of the first raw stages. Condolences can be given in person, by letter or by card.
- Unless you know someone very well, you should not phone them up to condole them. Bereavements always involve a vast amount of telephoning and organising

anyway and you are more likely to be a hindrance than a help.

- Condolences cannot be sent by e-mail and under no circumstances by text message.
- Don't worry too much about putting your foot in it. One letter of condolence said, 'Apart from this [death of wife], I hope everything is all right.' But it's unlikely you'd go to this extreme of ineptitude. Bereaved people are often forgiving or don't even notice an unfortunate remark. A nosy neighbour once said, 'I saw your husband going off in the ambulance this morning.' 'Yes, well, he died,' said the widow, who was later more concerned about her abrupt manner of breaking the news. Attempts to be cheerful might misfire: 'Never mind. In six months you'll be feeling a lot better.' (Implication: 'And have forgotten all about it'.) All you have to do is express regret and concern, then say what you valued or enjoyed about the dead person, which need not be anything very solemn or serious.
- Histrionic phrases – 'this terrible time', 'this overwhelming tragedy', 'your unbearable loss' – are not ideal.
- Some people would rather die than say 'death' or 'died' or any other variant. Why?

Acknowledging condolences

A staple feature of the letter of condolence is, 'Please don't think of replying.' But people almost always do.

- Individual replies are plainly ideal but there may well be circumstances in which this would be too overwhelming or distressing.
- If that is the case, you can send printed cards or put a notice in the paper.
- As for verbal condolences, although it is understandable that in a time of grief you might forget your manners, it is discouraging to the person, who might well have had to screw up their courage to speak at all, if the response is brusque or offhand.

Holiday Manners

Villa holidays

A lot of people go on villa holidays with their friends – and fall out. They say, 'Going on holiday is a real test of friendship.' They mean that their friends have failed.

Zoe has had, and been in, quite a lot of trouble over villa holidays. Usually, it's a party of ten, for economy reasons. There are arguments about absolutely everything – some are lazy but others are doing too much, taking over, suddenly self-appointed experts in whatever country they happen to be in. Or they've hogged the best room, made false claims about their contribution to the kitty, disputed what they should contribute to the kitty. Couples are at fault – too couply, not joining in. Zoe herself is something of a stirrer. She will be found in corners, trying to turn the slightly unfortunate overweight one who was her best friend back in Balham into the dustbin figure of the group.

Not a few times, after such a holiday, some of Zoe's friends have become former friends for good.

Yet often, people who don't know each other at all go on holiday and get along perfectly well. Foursomes or even larger groups are regularly to be seen on agreeable jaunts – and never a sharp word between them.

Why is this?

Why are some happy and some miserable? Is it really that Zoe and her nightmare gang, thrown together for two weeks, have discovered the 'truth' about each other? Or is it just that they don't know how to behave?

- It's the appalling stress of being on holiday, inflamed 1,000 per cent by the unhinged notion that they ought to be having a wonderful time, that turns normally reasonable, quite sane people into monsters, not some flaw in their personality. This is also what makes calm, easygoing people suddenly violently intolerant of the little foibles of others.

- Don't fall for any of that dream-holiday nonsense. The best you can hope for is a challenge which you might just about be able to meet. For some reason, foreign locations are often popular for holidays – which means, of course, too hot, horrible insects, can't make yourself understood, strong probability of getting ill, shops miles away and always closed. On top of that, you're on holiday, so you haven't got anything to do, not even a little bit of photo-copying.

- In other words, have the lowest possible expectations.

- Think ahead. The young never do this. If you must have a large group of ten or more, contemplate thoroughly beforehand the difficulties of feeding such a number – which will be considerable. It's no good thinking it'll just 'happen'. A smaller villa with fewer people might be a better choice.

- Avoid disputes about rooms by finding out in advance if they vary. It may be that some members of the group should pay less. The allocation of rooms can possibly be agreed on beforehand, especially if you can look at pictures of them on the Internet.

- Don't go on a villa holiday unless your main priority is to make the holiday a success. Don't be tempted by the low prices. In other words, you mustn't be selfish; you've got to be nice. Everybody knows how to be nice if they really want to. This is the time to remember what Quentin Crisp said: 'The well-mannered person ardently wants social relations to run smoothly.'

- Think carefully before you decide that a person is being

bossy. Just because somebody always does the shopping, it doesn't mean they are taking over the whole show. That may be their particular strength. Somebody else's expertise may be plumping the cushions and tidying around the swimming pool (should there be one). Often, accusations of bossiness are unfair.

- If a person refuses to let somebody else have a go or seems to be trying to turn the place into a boot camp, there might be a problem. Sometimes, people like this need to be soothed and reassured. Try to convince them that the world will not end if the washing-up isn't done by three o'clock.

- Don't expect a perfect division of labour. It's mean-spirited to get a ruler out and insist on exact quantifications of everybody's efforts. Just be grateful if people are *trying*.

- If somebody doesn't lift a finger, ask them nicely to do something quite specific. 'Would you mind doing . . . ?' If they kick up a fuss, explain what all the others have done and ask them if there's something else they would like to do. Be patient.

- It's very dismal if a villa party fragments – separate meals, separate outings. Not much point at all if people are, in fact, holidaying on their own with the rest of the villa party as faintly unwelcome background wadding. But couples, perhaps, or other smaller groups, might take themselves off somewhere on their own now and again. They shouldn't announce this as a unilateral decision, 'We're doing this . . .', but put it more gently, 'Would it be OK with everybody else if we . . . ?' They might invite others to come with them.

- Always try to be constructive and positive. Don't nurture resentments carefully behind people's backs. If someone is a bit sulky, say, 'What can we do to cheer you up?' Consider that you might have got the wrong end of the stick. Tim Hely Hutchinson, the publishing mogul, once awoke from his afternoon siesta in an Italian villa to find that his friends had all gone out and abandoned him. It was lucky he thought better of making a scene because it turned out that they'd been buying presents for him. This also shows us that even very grand people suffer slightly on villa holidays.
- If anybody really is unbearable, don't suffer in silence. Think of others. Sling them out – tell them it's for their own good.

See also **I must clean for the cleaner**, page 230.

Money Manners

Debts small and large, and Can we let them pay?

Money is dangerous. Nothing is better for generating ill feeling. Zoe complains, 'I've got this whole list of people who owe me £4.87 for a glass of wine and some peanuts, £7.50 for a cinema ticket, £4.80 for a taxi. They just never even mention it, unless you ask; then they look at you like you're mental and it's like, "Chill out, what's your problem?" Sometimes they say, "I've only got £3.50. Is that OK?" when they owe you £3.67. It's like a challenge. "Are you really going to be small-minded about 17p?" It's just so unfair.'

Zoe, normally so 'let it all hang out', doesn't put up with any nonsense when it comes to money. Maybe it's because she doesn't have very much. In PR, you are expected to subsist on glamour, not that there's a great deal of that.

And then there's splitting the bill in restaurants. Zoe's not a quibbler. She doesn't say, 'My main was £7.85 and yours was £9.90.' But she does say, 'Why do I have to pay the same if someone's had steak and a bottle of wine and I've only had a salad and a glass of water?'

Should you lend people more serious sums of money – not just tiding them over until they can get to the cash machine? Matt once lent an old school-friend £500 – and never saw it again. The late Jimmy Goldsmith believed that you should never lend people money – much better to give it to them instead. But he could talk, he was a multi-millionaire.

Finally, there are those who seem to avoid debts of any kind, who won't even let you pay. Matt wants to know, 'What do you do when you want to pay for something like some drinks and the other person keeps trying to force a fiver on you or whatever? They won't give up. You're saying, "No, really, let me pay," and they're saying, "No, no, I insist. Go on. Take it!" Sometimes it goes on for hours and it can get quite nasty.'

- If you owe somebody a small sum of money for a cinema ticket, drink or whatever, make a point of giving it to them at the earliest opportunity. People hate having to ask; it makes them feel mean.
- Better still, avoid having to borrow these small sums in the first place. Go to a cash machine and get your own supply.
- In restaurants, quibbling over the bill and insisting on paying only for what you had is absurd. Apart from anything else, the maths is so complicated, you'll never get out of the place.

- *But* there are exceptions, not often recognised. If someone has had a vastly more expensive dish than everybody else, or had something that nobody else had, such as an aperitif or a pudding, then why on earth shouldn't they pay for it? And it's their job to offer to do so.
- Only lend people money if you can afford never to see it again. People needing to borrow money from their friends have to be dodgy. Why can't they go to the bank or a mortgage company? If the person won't accept it as a gift, you would do well to *think* of it as such. Maybe you'll get it back, maybe you won't.
- If someone offers to pay, some token resistance is under-standable, but don't let the terrible dread of obligation (a low motive for resistance) crush the generous gesture. The person who offers to pay *first* should be allowed to do so, eventually.

Children's Manners – Mostly for Parents

Perfect dears

The child of forty years ago, in knee-length socks, answering politely when spoken to, holding doors open for grown-ups, fetching and carrying in the kitchen and asking to get down from the table, is now extinct. The modern child is an inert mogul who presides from the sofa, exercising absolute power over the remote control and only showing small signs of life when ordering snacks from the kitchen, which it does regularly for there must always be something to eat.

The other day, at Matt's home in Peterborough, his wife Lucy announced dinner (if you can call it that) to their three children, aged eight to fourteen. At their leisure they found convenient pausing places in their various computer games, then they all looked at their watches. 'What sort of time do you call this?' one of them said. In the kitchen the oldest one commented drily of his father, who was held up in his office, 'Maybe he's having an affair.' (Not very likely.)

Lucy had a girlfriend round; they were at one end of the table and the children at the other, so the young people were able to do what they like, which is keep conversation with adults to a minimum. Separate tables would be ideal, even when the poor old grandparents are over. However, on certain occasions, it's a different story. 'We went to a Christmas party last year,' says Matt, 'and our eldest, Ollie, who was only thirteen at the time, insisted on being given a bottle of beer and then went round the party introducing himself to people and carrying on conversations like he'd been doing it all his life. He was so confident it was rather appalling. Why wasn't he clinging onto his mummy like I used to do at that age?'

The thinking today is that children must never be made to feel inferior. In fact, they are to be treated as equals and more. Where adults, however vaguely, might be expected to make some effort with table manners, to hold doors open, to get up from their seats now and again, even in some circumstances to relinquish them altogether, children are totally exempt. How terrible it would be to force them to do anything. There must be no 'oughts' or 'shoulds'; they must be free, they must be themselves.

Then there is the matter of small children, babies and so on. Mrs Gibbs is not especially fond of small children. 'Is anybody, if the truth were told?' She has an unlikely ally in Zoe. 'I went round to a friend's for the evening and she made me bounce her horrible spotty baby on my knee. It wouldn't stop crying and after about half an hour my friend said, "You're not too popular, Zoe." There was nothing to eat, baby clobber everywhere, so nowhere to sit down. While the baby was up, which was until about ten, we weren't allowed to talk about anything else. Once it was asleep, we had to whisper.' Mrs Gibbs says, 'Babies aren't a suitable form of entertainment for adults.'

So, what shall we do? Turn the clock back? Children seen and only heard in the form of painful squeaky responses to inept adult interrogation, wetted-down hair, no cake until you've had your bread and butter? Grandmothers, like Matt's, muttering sternly in the grandson's ear, 'We certainly won't let Cousin Hugh know that you can't tell the difference between a buzzard and falcon'?

No. The over-trained, chronically polite children of yesterday were ghastly – really quite sinister and unnatural. But parents of today go too far in the opposite direction to avoid this fate, almost as far as neglect. To give no guidance, to have no expectations, is not what children want either. Children, with the exception of one or two stroppy adolescents ('adolescence' as commonly understood is a myth), are as anxious to avoid upsetting people as the rest of us.

- First and foremost, parents, don't fall for the 'adolesence' myth. Most teenagers are perfectly 'normal' or at least not traumatised and dysfunctional. Research has proved this. They are therefore quite capable of behaving reasonably; in fact, they probably want to.
- It is discouraging for visitors, especially revered relations such as grandparents, if children appear quite indifferent to their arrival – if they are unable to wrench themselves away from their computer games, unplug themselves from their iPods or switch off the TV.
- Older children may not wish to spend all their time in adult company, but the separatist regimes in place in many homes make no sense. Children gain confidence and knowledge from talking properly to adults. Parents, don't leave them in the prison of their own limitations. They should remain at the table throughout the meal and join in the conversation. Parents should coax them beyond offhand, monosyllabic answers.
- Liberate them from terrible snatching, grabbing and shovelling table manners.
- Parents of small children and babies, exhibit them or talk about them (or both) for a maximum of twenty minutes.
- There should be time for adults too.

For the matter of thank-you letters, see **Presents are different**, page 217.

Other people's children

'When I was a girl,' says Mrs Gibbs, 'I had a terrible habit of eavesdropping on the grown-ups. Whenever they looked up, there I was, lurking. My own mother could do nothing, but one day, her best friend suddenly went for me. "We've had quite enough of you," she said. "Go away and find something else to do." It was a terrible shock, of course, and certainly did the trick, I can tell you.'

Today it could not be more different. But there are many parents who, when they get their horns locked with their children, would benefit from a lightning strike such as that carried out by Mrs Gibbs's mother's friend.

But it is absolutely not done to interfere with other people's parenting. Parenting is now a 'skill' in which pride is taken. At the same time, the deep natural bonds between parent and child are revered as never before.

The result is that parents have no support. And children have no idea that it isn't just their bastard parents who expect them to avoid running up vast mobile phone bills.

- Why not intervene if other people's children are behaving badly? You take your life in your hands. But why not?

Letters and Cards Manners

Thank-you letters and cards for meals and parties – a major rethink

Some people say, 'You only have to write a thank-you letter if you've held a knife and fork in your hand.' But for others it's, 'Only if you've spent the night.'

The first rule means that you slave away trying to cover at least a side with effusions of thanks for a bit of quiche and a bought-in trifle, while for the hosts who have spent millions on champagne and those canapés that are always offered on what look like floor tiles with a miniature garden surrounding them – not a word.

A further confusion is that some people 'let it be known' that they expect a thank-you but others absolutely loathe them. 'If it's neatly folded napkins and thank-you notes afterwards, I'm not going,' says the novelist Sarah Long.

So nobody knows what to do, it's all down to individual hosts. 'In my family,' says Mrs Gibbs, 'they were called "Collinses" after the frightful Mr Collins in *Pride and*

Prejudice. They were a tremendous joke. I was always trying to make mine more obsequious and overdone than my sister's. I can't believe all these cards and notes flying about nowadays,' she adds. 'What a lot of fuss!'

Zoe does not usually send thank-you letters, but when she was going out, briefly, with that rich older man who has been mentioned before, she was told that she must and laboured for days to extend her paragraph on the melon-and-parma-ham starter to the bottom of the page.

And Matt has his guilty look. 'Lucy once found out that I'd got a backlog of about seven thank-yous. I really hate doing them and sometimes they're over six months late.'

- Let's put him out of his misery. Let's abolish the whole thing.
- No thank-you letters or cards for meals and parties – none of any kind.
- Written thank-yous are too formal. Nobody sends them to their real friends, the people they see all the time. But often you're trapped in this dreary grind of distancing thank-yous long after acquaintances have become real friends. Nobody on either side can bring themselves to say, 'Let's not bother.'
- Thanks at the door, which should be offered in such a way as the hosts will notice (not flung over your shoulder as you rush for the bus or jumbled up with the hysteria of rummaging for the car keys), are quite sufficient.
- You can also do quite a lot of thanking and appreciating *while the meal or party is going on.*

- If you feel that you've not thanked *enough*, as often happens, why not phone up? What is this terrible taboo on actually speaking to people who've invited you to their home? Or you can e-mail (so much easier to write a friendly and chatty e-mail than grind out a 'Collins'). Or, if you know the people very well, you can send a text message.
- Sometimes, a perfectly phrased thank-you card is plainly a substitute for ever asking back. But no amount of beautiful thanking will make up for *never being heard of again* (see **Do we dare to ask them back?**, page 132). Subsequent friendly contact of whatever kind (not, please, the ghastly tit-for-tat of 'it's our turn') is what really matters.

Thanking if you've been to stay

There are various kinds of going to stay. Matt laments the lack of people to stay with. A colleague 'relocated' to Bath and a visit has been much discussed but has never taken place. Otherwise, the only staying he does is with his rich friend in various superb holiday villas in Tuscany, Greece and Spain. Zoe once went to stay with the parents of a girlfriend who lived in what she described as a 'stately home' but it wasn't really. She did begin an epic Collins, but it was never finished, let alone sent.

- Mostly, people stay with people they know well. You might take a present and thank by phone or e-mail.
- If friends invite you to their holiday villa at their own

expense, offer to make a contribution – take them out to dinner, offer to pay for food shopping. And buy them a present.

- If you stay with people you don't know very well or at all (the parents of a friend perhaps), you should write a letter to thank, unless they have been exceptionally friendly and perhaps supplied their e-mail address.
- I have heard of people who take offence at the lack of a thank-you letter after another kind of 'staying over' i.e. after a one-night stand. This is bizarre. What are you supposed to say? Are general comments on the bedroom decor sufficient? Or should you be more thorough, taking in the sheets, pillows etc. ('Egyptian cotton is always my favourite')? Or are you just supposed to be pornographic? Until these questions have been settled, we can safely say that thank-yous for one-night stands need not be sent.

Presents are different

Writing Christmas thank-yous was an agony of most pre-1980s childhoods, almost on a level with being made to eat corned beef and not being allowed to have cake before the bread and butter.

Modern children sit with their calculators on Christmas morning and on their birthdays. If the total value of their presents comes to anything less than £1,000, there's all hell to pay. Even more astonishing – they have been let off writing thank-you letters altogether!

Mrs Gibbs is stoical. 'The worst of it is, you don't even

know if they got the wretched thing. I thought about stinging letters for some of my non-thanking great-nieces and -nephews but in the end there was a more straightforward solution – cross them off my Christmas-present list!'

Some adults are slack about thanking, too. Rarely is it because they are riddled with strange scruples and embarrassment like the two ladies in Proust who agonised for days about how to thank Monsieur Swann for a case of wine. In the end, one of them dropped into the conversation, 'Some people have such nice neighbours.' That was it!

- Presents must be thanked for in some shape or form. It would be wrong for givers to expect grovelling gratitude, but, as Mrs Gibbs says, they want to know that their present hasn't been lost in the post. In any case, receivers of gifts surely wish to acknowledge the kind thought of the giver in some way?

- Presents can be thanked for there and then, when they are opened – provided, of course, that the giver is present. Often people feel that they have not thanked enough or, upon reflection, there is something more they want to say about the gift – in which case they can e-mail, telephone or write. A letter of thanks for a present will never create the slightly chilly effect of the postal Collins for dinner or a party.

- Children should be encouraged to thank properly – not just a few words mumbled into the floor – and if their efforts are inadequate, they should write, e-mail or telephone subsequently.

Christmas cards

Zoe is horrid about Christmas cards and refuses to send any at all, Matt and Lucy run a highly efficient dispatch service, and Mrs Gibbs begins early in December and writes reams and reams in each one. 'It's a marvellous way to keep in touch when you're my age and you've got friends all over the country you never see from one year to the next. I usually get ones back with a nice bit of news. Occasionally, it's just 'Happy Christmas'. If that goes on for a few years, I cross them off my list.'

Matt was traumatised once when he received a card from one of his commuting mates: 'It arrived on the twenty-third so it was too late to send one back.' Then there's the whole agonising question of whether they should be addressed to all the children in the family as well.

- Christmas cards are always appreciated by the recipient, however much of a labour it might be to send them. Don't listen to the groaners and moaners who say, 'What's the point, we see them all the time?' or, 'What's the point, we never see them?'
- Cards for people you never see should contain a bit of news and some message beyond 'Happy Christmas'. It need only be a few sentences.
- People don't send cards just to get one back. Or they shouldn't. One writer (they are odd people) keeps a careful list of who he has sent cards to. He ticks them off as

cards are returned and any left unticked are delisted the next year. This is appalling.

- Children have no interest in receiving cards from their parents' fuddy-duddy friends. They are either too young to notice (absurd to send them to babies) or far too busy sending cards to about a hundred thousand of their closest friends.
- Christmas cards should *never* be sent by e-mail. Apart from anything else, where's the card?

Round-robin letters

The round-robin Christmas message has recently surged in popularity; a lot of unkind things have been said. Lucy is quite keen to send one but Matt has so far managed to prevent her. 'How would it go? "Another excellent year for the Lawson family!!!!" Then a lot of boasting about the children's GCSE results and where we've been on holiday and what health problems we've had.'

Zoe thinks round-robin letters are naff and disgusting. Mrs Gibbs doesn't like them either.

A round-robin letter doesn't have to be packed with clichés, exclamation marks and false bonhomie. Although they often are. They say things like, 'Upgraded to a Mégane in July. The Bentley will have to wait until next year!!!!' or, 'Ten more swimming badges to add to the Mumford family archive!' One round robin I heard of was written in a terrifying confessional mode. It spared no details of the teenage daughter's unwanted pregnancy by a middle-aged, married

Uzbekistani meatpacker at Tesco's. All recipients were pain-
fully embarrassed.

There might be some debate. Are round-robin letters bad
taste or bad manners?

- Round-robin letters are impersonal by definition.
- A really good letter engages in some way with the person
  addressed – it is not just the writer expounding on the
  subject of themselves. But a round robin is not addressed
  to an individual. The writer/s can only write about themselves (or some tiresome cause they've got hold of).
  How can a round robin avoid self-importance and even
  boasting?
- A few carefully chosen sentences written on a Christmas
  card might speak more to the recipient than yards and
  yards of round robin.

Presents and Gifts Manners

Presents: It's the thought that counts

Or is it? There is much bitterness about presents. 'When I got married,' says Mrs Gibbs, 'I lived in dread of being given a Susie Cooper teaset. Lo and behold, that's exactly what I got. It was years and years before it all got broken.' A colleague of Zoe's complained and complained about her job. Zoe said, 'Why don't you leave?' 'Oh, no, I might get a really naff leaving present like a pashmina or one of those water-filter jugs.' The ingratitude!

What to give? What to do with what is given? Evelyn Waugh said that once the servants had left, he could finally throw away all the presents they had ever given him.

Can we stop people giving us presents? Do we want to? At Christmas there will inevitably be an assault. And people under the age of about fifty-five actually like presents, however much they complain about them. Their birthdays wouldn't be the same without them. In recent years, especially for 'big' birthdays, presents have become more and more of a feature. A competitive element has crept in. Usually, at the party a special place is designated for all the Prada, Burberry, Botega Veneta and Jimmy Choo bags to be piled up.

People like Matt spend many of their Saturday evenings at birthday parties (it's either that or a Christmas party or a summer party). 'These days you've just got to take a present. You can have a really hard time thinking of something,' he complains.

- You've got to take a present to a birthday party.
- You can prevent an attack of presents by putting on the invitation, 'No Presents' (an instruction that should always be obeyed). This is noble and self-sacrificing.
- Never think, 'They're rich. We'd better spend £100.' Spend what you can afford or less. If a vase from a junk shop costs 10p but is absolutely beautiful (and the person likes such things), then it is the perfect present.

- Boring presents are best, especially for people you don't know so well. Mrs Gibbs's mother used to knit dishcloths which made very acceptable and practical presents. What's wrong with wine, champagne, book tokens, subscriptions to magazines, towels, sheets, olive oil, sensible foods, vases, bowls, soap? These are things people will actually use or can never have enough of.
- Better than useless gimmicks and oddities – verjuice, pomegranate essence, a keyring with aspirin holder, a candle scented with fig and black pepper, or a set of chocolate moulds for the next time you're making your own chocs.

Do I bring a bottle?

Anxiety about this seems to be mounting amongst the over thirties. For Matt it's a big worry. He complains of odd looks from hosts. Hosts seem to be bewildered. It's strange because not so long ago everybody appeared to know exactly where they stood. But now the idea is taking root that bringing a bottle is some kind of insult, implying that your hosts are poor or don't have very nice wine. It must have something to do with our increased affluence.

- What a lot of nonsense. It's a gift. It can only be an insult if it's something utterly filthy which the guest is wanting to get rid of.
- Hosts, however rich you are or however proud of your own wine cellar, please don't be surprised or bewildered

at the proffered bottle. Try to receive it graciously and matter of factly (it'll probably be in its bag from the off-licence, so it doesn't call for as much fuss as a 'proper' present tied up with ribbon).

- Once you've got it, you can do what you like with it. You're not obliged to offer it. If it turns out that your guests only brought it because it's what they wanted to have themselves, then you're entitled to feel offended. At Anthony Powell's eightieth-birthday party, Roy Jenkins hid the bottle of Château Latour he had brought beside the fridge, thinking to keep it for himself. But he got caught. (This story also proves that the very grandest people bring bottles.)
- The custom of taking presents – or maybe they should be called 'offerings' – to hosts is a pleasant one. Let's keep it up! A bottle of wine is the best choice – easy to obtain

and most likely to be welcome. Chocolates are a bit fussy, aren't they, in their little gold boxes – and they don't cost as much. Flowers might be appreciated in the long run but Matt complains of 'the hassle of working out what to do with them while you've got all the other host stuff to do'. He's not very grateful, is he?

Dog Manners

Such a lovely dog!

'I'm not very fond of dogs,' says Mrs Gibbs. 'Years ago, I was having a drink with our doctor. When I got up, the dog had eaten my skirt.' What, all of it? 'Not quite. The doctor was most unhelpful. He said I should have noticed.'

Worse things could happen. On arrival at the family home of the writer Peter Parker, a visiting Pekinese was snapped in half by one of the Parker Labradors. This cast rather a pall over the ensuing lunch. In 2003, the Queen's Christmas was wrecked when her daughter, Princess Anne, drew up at the door of Sandringham with her killer bull terrier, Dotty. Within seconds, Her Majesty's favourite corgi had been mauled to death. You wonder if Anne will be asked again.

'What do you do, in polite company, if dogs are . . . you know . . . at it?' asks Matt. But Zoe is more annoyed by dog-owner friends who seem to think the one thing she craves is a bouncy Dalmatian jumping up all over her, slobbering and covering her cardigan with its hairs.

- Dog owners, don't let that dog out of your sight for a second.
- Don't assume that everybody will love your dog as you do. Someone I know dumped her boyfriend because he was always trying to make her cuddle his dog.

- If dogs are copulating in full view, humans do not refer to it.
- If you want to take your dog to someone else's home, you must always ask. But the answer must always be yes.

Staff Manners – Mainly for Punters and Employers

Waiter! Waiter!

Zoe's rich boyfriend, the one who made her cook a bridge supper, was horrid to waiters. 'Waiter!' he would call. 'Over here, please. I want my steak *à point*. Have you got that? . . . This salt's damp. That's a good start, isn't it?'

It's instantly recognisable, the not-being-very-nice-to-waiters mode. In the end, for Zoe, it was a good enough reason to ditch him. For others, starting out, the treatment of the waiter might be crucial. 'We used to get rid of a man if on the first date he was beastly to the waiters,' says Mrs Gibbs. 'Some of them thought they were being grand and we'd be impressed. Not a bit of it. It was a good test. It was either that or whether they were afraid of wasps.'

Is it advisable to swing the other way? To be matey? 'Hi, how are you? Great to see you. I'd like to be your guest. What do you suggest we order?'

Not really.

- Don't call the waiter 'Waiter!'
- 'Please,' and 'Thank you,' 'Do you think I could . . . ?' 'I wonder if you could . . .' No peremptory commands.
- No mateyness either. Waiters find this embarrassing.

I must clean for the cleaner

A lot of people are frightened of their cleaners. Perhaps with reason. If displeased, indoor staff can wreak havoc. Look at Paul Burrell, nearly bringing down the monarchy. Years ago, a stuck-up gentleman told the maid to provide finger bowls at dinner. When he sailed into the dining parlour with his important guests (whoever they were) he found towels and bars of carbolic soap laid on as well. Another woman I know had an exceptionally hefty cleaning woman who said, when asked to dust the tops of the doors, 'You do your job, I'll do mine.'

Watch out!

The trouble is that fear is all tangled up with dissatisfaction. Our cleaners don't clean enough. 'I've got this very nice girl now,' says Mrs Gibbs. 'She's from Central Europe. But she doesn't know the first thing about cleaning – no elbow, no idea of polishing – or how to make a bed – no hospital corners. And she won't touch anything but those very expensive Duchy of Cornwall biscuits. You see, I was spoiled for years with Mrs Clatworthy who'd been trained as a housemaid and knew how to sweep out a bread oven.'

But the temper of cleaners and dislike of criticism are legendary.

Zoe has fallen out with quite a few who have come to work in her chaotic flat share in Balham. The cleaners, according to Zoe, never got anything done. She didn't trust them.

Matt's difficulty, on the other hand, is financial. Should he pay the cleaner for holidays? Should he give her extra at Christmas? 'My rich friend, Matthew, pays his for all her holidays and gives her £50 at Christmas. To be honest, I'd find it a stretch to do that.'

- Be realistic in your expectations! Zoe's cleaners are expected to clean the whole, untidy flat in two hours. It's no wonder they get in a muddle. Posh Spice, Mrs David Beckham, is said to have 'poshed her butler too far' (*News of the World* speak). According to the newspaper, it was a killing strain organising Romeo's second birthday, on top of his daily chores. Then he was asked to do the christening. It was too much. He had to quit.
- Give precise instructions about what you want done and how (what cleaning materials, methods to be used etc.). Write this down for the cleaner.
- Constantly ask the cleaner if the tasks are manageable in the time.
- If something has not been well cleaned, say, 'That cooker is terribly difficult to clean, I know. Could you have another go?' Or, 'Maybe it would be easier if you did it like this . . .'
- Praise and thank the cleaner for what has been done well. 'My goodness, the kitchen was sparkling last week! I think you gave it everything you've got.'

- Agree when you engage your cleaner whether or not you are going to pay for holidays.
- A Christmas bonus is uncalled for. It's a tip (see **Tipping**, page 19).

Other staff

Other staff are not really staff. A lot of people engage personal trainers, stylists, food stylists, floral artists, lifestyle managers. These people are business associates, although, if they are Carole Caplin, they can unwittingly do a lot of harm. As with Cherie Blair, it is usual to regard them as friends. They are invited to sit down, join you at meals etc. Many builders are now on these sorts of terms with their 'clients'.

Afterword

Quentin Crisp said that nothing is more likely to drive a person into a monastery than an etiquette book: 'There are so many trivial ways in which it is possible to commit some social sin.' I hope this is not how you feel after reading this book. Manners *should* make you feel more yourself.

But this is easier said than done. A health warning is called for. Manners can ruin your life, make you hysterical, unhinge you, cause you to lose your grip on reality altogether. Be careful that you never reach the point where all you see in other people are their manners or you'll end up like Lady Redesdale, the mother of the Mitford sisters, who declared barkingly that Hitler was all right because he 'had such charming manners'.

Or standards can be *too* ferociously high. There is a terrifying story of the writer, André Gide. He had dinner with a friend in a restaurant in Paris. The friend left a mean tip. By design, Gide left his umbrella behind. Out in the street he said, 'Oh, dear, I've left my umbrella behind,' went back into the restaurant, waylaid the undertipped waiter, and said, 'My friend is mortified. He got his coins muddled up and now he realises he didn't leave you enough. Here's some more.'

To some, this demonstrates perfect manners. Nobody was offended or shown up. Others may wonder how the penny-pinching friend was to learn. In any case, it's hard to see how someone who put so much effort into his manners could ever have had time for anything else.

Manners are making a comeback, by public demand as much as anything else. You only have to mention the subject and people come alive. The media takes an eager interest. This is excellent. As we know, the right sort of manners make sense, encourage kindness and consideration, help the shy and ill at ease to feel more comfortable. But still we must guard against overdoing it. We don't want the air turning blue (or purple?) as we all take to disapproving of each other's manners. We don't want people trapping themselves in a terrible prison of daintiness and artificial behaviour through excessive preoccupation with their own manners. We have to be tolerant and easygoing. If we want other people to have better manners, we'll have to encourage this in a joshing way, with good humour and subtlety. We should not be too quick to judge other people's manners, anyway. Being late once or twice, or now and again texting under the table during dinner, is not absolute evidence of monstrous selfishness. Modern manners should follow the example of the Catholic faith. Intermittent lapses can always be forgiven. It is the intention that matters.

So, let's usher in a new age of modern manners.